THE PITCHING EDGE

SECOND EDITION

Tom House, PhD

Human Kinetics

Library of Congress Cataloging-in-Publication Data

House, Tom, 1947-
  The pitching edge / Tom House. — 2nd ed.
      p.   cm.
  Includes index.
  ISBN 0-7360-0155-7
  1. Pitching (Baseball)   I. Title.
GV871.H52   1999
796.357'22—dc21   99-18237

ISBN-10: 0-7360-0155-7
ISBN-13: 978-0-7360-0155-7

Developmental Editor: Kent Reel; **Assistant Editor:** Kim Thoren; **Copyeditor:** Dan Amerman; **Proofreader:** Bob Replinger; **Graphic Designer:** Robert Reuther; **Graphic Artist:** Kimberly Maxey; **Art Manager:** Craig Newsom; **Photo Editor:** Clark Brooks; **Cover Designer:** Jack W. Davis; **Photographer (cover):** Ron Vesely; **Photographer (interior):** Photos on pages iii, 1, 109 © Rob Tringali, Jr./SportsChrome USA; III, 53 © 1999 Joe Robbins; 7, 17 © SportsChrome USA; 105, 115, 121 © Michael Zito/SportsChrome USA; 133 © Greg Crisp/SportsChrome USA; 125 © Anthony Neste; **Illustrator:** Keith Blomberg; **Printer:** United Graphics.

Human Kinetics books are available at special discounts for bulk purchase. Special editions or book excerpts can also be created to specification. For details, contact the Special Sales Manager at Human Kinetics.

Printed in the United States of America   10

Human Kinetics
Web site: www.HumanKinetics.com

United States: Human Kinetics, P.O. Box 5076, Champaign, IL 61825-5076
800-747-4457
e-mail: humank@hkusa.com

Canada: Human Kinetics, 475 Devonshire Road, Unit 100, Windsor, ON N8Y 2L5
800-465-7301 (in Canada only)
e-mail: orders@hkcanada.com

Europe: Human Kinetics, 107 Bradford Road, Stanningley
Leeds LS28 6AT, United Kingdom
+44 (0) 113 255 5665
e-mail: hk@hkeurope.com

Australia: Human Kinetics, 57A Price Avenue, Lower Mitcham, South Australia 5062
08 8372 0999
e-mail: liaw@hkaustralia.com

New Zealand: Human Kinetics, Division of Sports Distributors NZ Ltd.
P.O. Box 300 226 Albany, North Shore City, Auckland
0064 9 448 1207
e-mail: info@humankinetics.co.nz

CONTENTS

FOREWORD

The University of Southern California baseball program has a proud history that's rich in championships on the field but equally rich in personal growth and achievement off the field.

It has always been my goal to coach our athletes to believe in preparation and hard work: that it was important being part of a *team* that won games, not just being the best player, and that a player who developed his mind as well as his body invariably increased his chances of success in a team effort.

As a pitcher at USC, Tom was an overachiever who may have been a little short on physical tools but long on work ethic and game smarts. He always found a way to compete. This knack carried over into his pro career both as a player and a coach. As an author, he shares his education, his research, and his experience. He's found new and better ways to develop physical and mental mound skills. Better preparation always increases the chances for success in competition.

In baseball, and in life, the mind sometimes wanders and the attention span lessens. Five decades of Trojan players will remember my phrase, "Tiger! What time is it?" (My way to bring mind and body back into focus.) Well, Tiger, it's time to read *The Pitching Edge*. You'll see that Tom has provided plenty of information, instruction, and inspiration—all you need to do is add the hard work. And, finally, Tiger, remember that good things happen when you throw strikes!

Rod Dedeaux
NCAA Division I Coach of the Century

PREFACE

As a major-league pitcher, coach, and an international baseball consultant, I have had little confidence in traditional word-of-mouth advice about pitching. Some of the coaching I hear makes sense, but more often than not the advice is contradictory and doesn't answer questions objectively. In getting and giving instruction on pitching, I've had vague, uneasy feelings about some of the information. This dissonance is the motivation behind my continuing efforts to improve the quality of both information and instruction for pitchers and coaches.

There are always better, more systematic ways to learn pitching and to observe and teach pitchers. I share this approach in revising *The Pitching Edge*, bringing physics-based, three-dimensional motion analysis from the laboratory to the mound more efficiently than in the original edition.

This book is the cutting-edge resource for objective information on pitching. It identifies and quantifies the significant performance improvement that is possible if you apply its contents. You won't have to decipher a lot of scientific mumbo-jumbo to understand the information. Some of the terms used to explain things may be new to you, though, because much of what you will be reading about didn't exist five years ago!

This new and improved information excites me as a researcher and motivates me as a coach. It is presented just as I teach it around the world: to Little Leaguers in the United States; to professional players in Japan; and to high school, college, and professional players in the United States.

If you are an athlete or a coach, you are sure to benefit from the information. In fact, those who work with pitchers—exercise physiologists, biomechanists, strength and conditioning trainers, even parents—will find information they can use. Quite simply, the information in *The Pitching Edge* revision has been further debugged. No other book synthesizes computer-generated video data analyses of contemporary major-league pitchers, more than 25 years of practical experience (8 as a major-league pitcher, 17 as a coach), and more than 15 years of research applied to the biomechanical, mental, nutritional, and physical conditioning of pitchers from 8 to 45 years old. In other words, *I've* made the mistakes that *you* don't have to!

The book is organized into three Ts for optimal pitching performance: technique, training, and thinking. I emphasize the biomechanical components of technique because this domain has been the least understood by athlete and coach and, as a result, causes more frustration and failure than necessary. The revised *Pitching Edge* will help you more than ever to take the guesswork out of pitching mechanics and provide the protocols and drills to correct flaws in any pitcher's delivery.

In part I, I share what new research and experience have determined is the most mechanically efficient and effective way to deliver a ball to the plate. In part II, you will find newer and better methods for conditioning the pitcher's total body and throwing arm. As a bonus, there are contributions from some of the leading baseball researchers to further broaden your information base. Finally, in part III, I focus on the mental aspects of pitching. Mental and emotional conditioning ultimately determine whether mechanical and physical training pay off in competition.

Every pitcher looks for an edge. Successful pitchers maximize their competitive edge with proper preparation—biomechanical, physical, nutritional, and mental. The revised *Pitching Edge* will inform, instruct, and inspire athletes and coaches to achieve optimum performance at any level of competition.

ACKNOWLEDGMENTS

Thanks to Alan Blitzblau, my longtime friend and fellow researcher at Bio-Kinetics. He always seems to find the right answers. Thanks to Bob Keyes and Dan Moffet, my new baseball buddies and fellow researchers at Bio-Kinetics. They are typical of the younger generation of sports science thinkers, not stuck with convention, willing to change the paradigm, and not afraid to push the envelope with me and my generation of coaches. Thanks to Dr. Tony Stellar: Bio-Kinetics could not have survived without his financial backing over the last 10 years. And, thanks, finally, to baseball. It's been good and it's been bad, but it's never been boring.

INTRODUCTION

The first edition of *The Pitching Edge* predicted that we would soon achieve a resolution between traditional baseball teachings and contemporary sports science. And since that book went into print back in 1994, subjective experience and objective information have been much more effectively integrated into the game. As a result, more people than ever agree on what pitchers should do to optimize their technique, training, and thinking. That information is slowly being shared and used throughout all levels of baseball. Step one accomplished.

Step two is less revolutionary but equally important. Whereas step one was a movement toward consensus, the second step—launched with this new edition of *The Pitching Edge*—is to gain a deeper understanding by answering three fundamental questions:

- What essential mechanics do winning pitchers, past and present, have in common?
- How do the most powerful and enduring pitchers train and care for their bodies and arms for peak performance and health?
- What makes a pitcher, mentally and emotionally, into a consistent winning pitcher?

Answers to these questions will allow us to account for the dilemmas we encounter every season in watching pitchers perform. For example, while it's obvious why Randy Johnson's 95 mph fastball is so effective, what makes Greg Maddux's 85 mph fastball equally as effective? Also, while it's great to be built like Kevin Brown, body shape alone didn't make Kevin the National League leader in ERA in 1997. How then do we explain Fernando Valenzuela, who in his prime pitched very successfully with the body of a middle-aged beer-league softballer? And, why did Sandy Koufax's elbow go bad at age 32, while Nolan Ryan pitched healthy into his mid-40s? Perhaps most perplexing is how an underwhelming physical specimen like Tony Fossas can pitch so tough in so many crucial situations, while an amazing physical talent like Sean Bergman struggles to make the key pitches and win the key games.

This revised edition of *The Pitching Edge* will better answer these questions concerning talent, skill, injury, and competition. The book will reveal what the game's best pitchers do physically and mentally when they deliver a baseball. Quantified answers will come from a broader base of on-the-field data using objective information, digitized and diagnosed with computerized, three-dimensional motion analysis. There will also be updated instructional protocols to complement this objective information.

I've revised and added to the "pitching absolutes," not because the information provided previously by the computer analyses was incorrect, but because I failed to ask the computer the right questions. Oftentimes, even at 1000 frames per second, I didn't know what to look for! Now I do, and I have. In this book you will get better information and instruction derived from better data and more experience with which to diagnose it.

The updated model still allows stylistic interpretations. We've identified five common factors involved in *technique,* six common factors to be integrated into *training*, and four common factors that are critical to pitchers' *thinking.*

A pitcher absorbs energy, directs energy, and delivers energy from feet to fingertips out and into a baseball. It's a process that sequentially loads the body's muscles in kinetic energy links, and these muscles must be trained for function to deliver energy efficiently. In part I, I'll explain and show in detail how each essential element of technique contributes to pitching success.

Part II provides proven training prescriptions for maximum performance and long-term health. Although not as comprehensive as the training program found in my book *Fit to Pitch* (see ordering information in the back of this book), the important functional fitness protocols specific to pitching are presented in clear and precise detail. Flat-ground work, competitive pitching loads, and between-start activities are just a few of the many areas covered on physical preparation.

Pitching techniques and training are useful only if the athlete's mental and emotional make up is sound. As that wise philosopher Yogi Berra once said, "50 percent of baseball is 90 percent mental." Effective thinking and emotional control are critical to the short- and long-term success of any pitcher. In part III you'll see how to master the mental aspects of pitching, thereby allowing the physical potential to be realized.

As in the first edition, information and instruction for coaches and players will be presented through text, photographs, illustrations, and three-dimensional stick figures. Special sections labeled "House Calls" offer corrective prescriptions; "House Rules" feature instructional tenets; and "Drills for Skills" provide practice protocols.

Just one more thing before you begin part I. Take time to examine the figure titled "The Science and Art of Pitching Competitively." This schematic shows how sports science, medical science, and coaching can contribute to a pitcher's precompetition preparation as well as his competitive performance. This book continues to combine the best information from each of these fields to help give you the pitching edge.

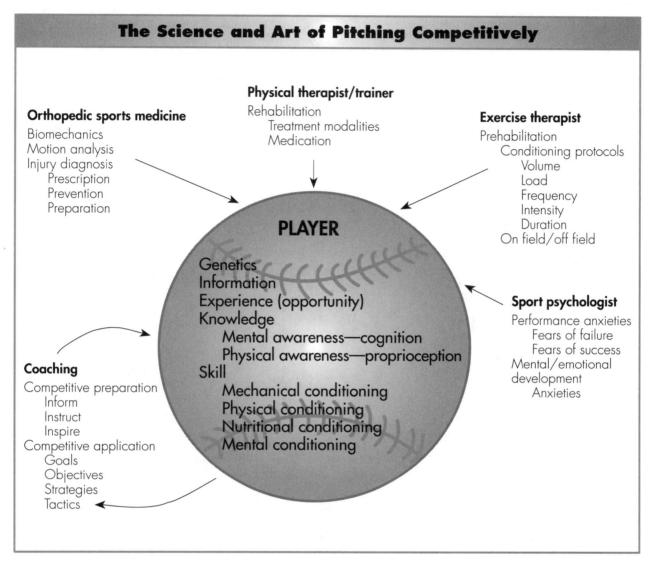

The Science and Art of Pitching Competitively

Physical therapist/trainer
Rehabilitation
   Treatment modalities
   Medication

Orthopedic sports medicine
Biomechanics
Motion analysis
Injury diagnosis
   Prescription
   Prevention
   Preparation

Exercise therapist
Prehabilitation
   Conditioning protocols
      Volume
      Load
      Frequency
      Intensity
      Duration
On field/off field

PLAYER
Genetics
Information
Experience (opportunity)
Knowledge
   Mental awareness—cognition
   Physical awareness—proprioception
Skill
   Mechanical conditioning
   Physical conditioning
   Nutritional conditioning
   Mental conditioning

Sport psychologist
Performance anxieties
   Fears of failure
   Fears of success
Mental/emotional
development
   Anxieties

Coaching
Competitive preparation
   Inform
   Instruct
   Inspire
Competitive application
   Goals
   Objectives
   Strategies
   Tactics

Pitchers have numerous resources available as they develop their genetic talent into optimal levels of skill. Note the mix of objective and subjective input—the science and art of pitching—plus the interdependent relationship of coach and player as they prepare for competition.

PART I

THE FIVE ABSOLUTES OF TECHNIQUE

"There are biomechanical imperatives and biomechanical inevitabilities. Master the imperative, let the inevitable happen."

Pitching technique has been taught for a hundred years. During the first 90 years of baseball, coaches used their own visual experience in combination with word-of-mouth tips to teach their pitchers. This trial and error continued until the mid- to late '70s, when professional coaches adapted video technology to instructional techniques. In the last five years, scouting and coaching have begun to integrate three-dimensional computerized motion analysis into the procurement and development of players. I'm predicting motion analysis technology will be the norm by the first decade of the new millenium.

The best coaches are usually three-dimensional thinkers. And the best pitchers always develop styles that work efficiently in three dimensions. There remains, however, much room for improvement in the learning process between instructors and athletes. Information gets nowhere without instruction.

COACH VS. PITCHER PERSPECTIVE

There always has been a gap between coach and pitcher—an information gap caused by misinterpretation of what a coach sees and says and what a pitcher feels and does. "Instructors see and teach; athletes feel and perform." I try to clarify this communication process with this statement: "These are my words. It is up to you to put a feeling to them." It seems to bridge some of the gap. Also, many coaches have taught the right thing but for the wrong reason. They knew what they wanted to see but they didn't know why or how. I've often heard good instructors say, "I don't know exactly what it is, but I'll recognize it when I see it!" This creates another gap between coach and pitcher. Too many say, "Try this . . . no, that's not it . . . Try that . . . no, not quite." It can be very frustrating.

Today, however, the high-tech combination of video and computer can provide coaches with objective biomechanical feedback. This bridges the gap significantly, shortening instructor and athlete learning curves by matching up the what and the why of pitching a baseball.

A final bridge in the communication between coach and pitcher is what biomechanists call proprioception. It's an inner feeling. An awareness of where the body or body part is in space. Athletes learn by hearing, seeing, and feeling. Feeling is the most efficient of the three. So, whenever possible, I will provide drills with specific implements to train the feeling for whatever position or movement I'm trying to get a pitcher to accomplish. It really helps the mastery of proper muscle memory.

In the next five chapters, I will expand on technique and the information and instruction exchange so necessary in player development. I will show how every coach and every pitcher can access the right mechanic for the right reason. As mentioned in the introduction, the format is model oriented and prioritized according to the sequence of movement a pitcher must accomplish to facilitate the integration of talent and skill. Extended research into an expanded database reveals five biomechanical abso-

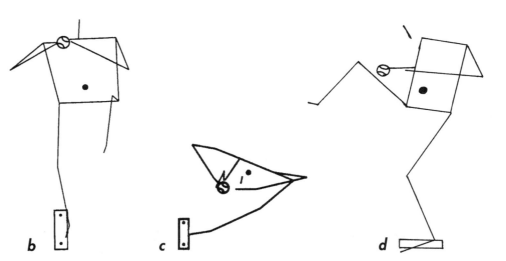

◆ **Figure I.1, a–d**   All four views show the pitcher at the same point in his delivery but from different perspectives.

lutes common to successful and healthy pitchers: (1) dynamic balance, (2) postural stabilization, (3) elbow alignment at foot strike, (4) late torso rotation, and (5) flex-T elbow position at release point. Each "absolute" will be addressed in a dedicated chapter. Each chapter will provide information and instruction for coaches or pitchers to improve their work on skills in preparation, as well as skill in competition. And always remember that with throwing workloads a pitcher is only as efficient as his worst biomechanical imperative. Biomechanical inefficiency invariably ends in poor performance or injury.

To complement the text, I've included illustrations or computer generated stick figures to model specific components of a pitcher's delivery (see figure I.1).

Take time to compare how all the visuals relate, especially the stick figures, and be patient with the perception of all three stick-figure views. When I first started motion analysis everything looked like spiders, and it was very difficult to determine right, left, front, back, top, or bottom! Here is the diagram I used to train my eyes (see figure I.2). In front view analysis, assume you are the catcher.

Now that you are an expert, you're ready for chapters 1 through 5. Good luck and good reading!

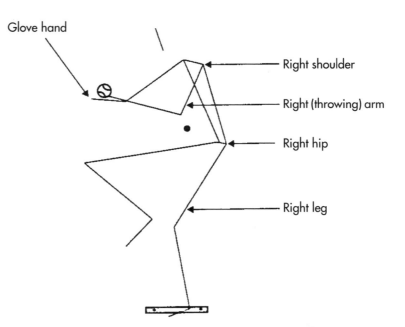

◆ **Figure I.2**   Here is the catcher's view of the pitcher. Use this diagram to train your eyes to understand the stick figures used in this book.

CHAPTER 1

Dynamic Balance

"Tom, I throw harder when I lift my leg higher.
Go put that in your computer!"
Nolan Ryan, 1989

Nolan Ryan had just finished a skill session in Arlington Stadium and was using his "country common sense" as a foil for my "science stuff." It was Nolan's first year with the Rangers and my fourth as the Rangers' pitching coach. Our dialogues on pitching were getting as competitive as some of his games. His intuitions were challenging not only because of his status as baseball's ultimate power pitcher but because it forced us to ask questions.

When I say *us*, I mean me and my partners at Bio-Kinetics, a computerized motion analysis firm in Salt Lake City, Utah. My "go to" guy in those days was Alan Blitzblau, our biomechanist and programmer. Alan baselined all BioKinetics hardware and software and taught me more about human movement than any baseball coach has. His two favorite phrases are these: "Let's ask the system what it thinks" and, "Maybe a better question will give us a better answer." Nolan's statement about his leg lift met the favorite-phrase criteria and got me more than a little curious to find out if what he felt was indeed true. I called Alan, explained the hypothesis, and asked for some quick computer analysis. Here is what he discovered.

Nolan's left leg was 19 percent of his total body weight. By lifting it six inches higher, Nolan recruited approximately 3 percent more potential energy into his body's energy system before starting toward home plate. This translated more energy up through his body when his landing foot hit, giving him more arm speed and power to put on his pitches. How much more? About 2 mph on his fastball. Nolan, as usual, was right. But Nolan's strength and flexibility were unique. He could keep perfect balance with the higher lift, something most pitchers can't do. So a high leg lift worked for Nolan, but many pitchers couldn't benefit from the technique because it would adversely affect their dynamic balance.

BALANCING THE DELIVERY

Balance is a prerequisite for efficiency in any human movement. Dynamic balance is especially important to pitchers as they stride down the mound, trying to coordinate lower body direction with feet and legs, while maintaining upper body direction and rotation with hips, torso, and arms to deliver a ball. "Dynamic" is a key word because balance through the pitching motion is not a static or a start/stop thing. Simply put, dynamic balance is controlling one's center of gravity (c.g.) from first movement to last in the windup and stretch. For many years, pitching coaches (me included) taught "stop at the top" or a "beat of balance" during leg lift into stride, mostly to prevent "rushing." It was not a good instruction. Laws of inertia tell us that an object in motion wants to remain in motion. Any pitcher who breaks up his body's momentum, once he has initiated movement to deliver a baseball, is fighting kinetic energy. And, as you'll see in successive chapters, pausing at the top of leg lift does not cure any one pitching illness; it falsely addresses a symptom, what we pitching coaches used to think was rushing (discussed in chapter 4).

Balance through the pitching motion is not static, but dynamic. Successful pitchers, such as David Cone, maintain their center of gravity in a balanced position from the first movement to the last.

The windup and stretch are really the same physical movement once the ball of the pivot foot is planted in front of the rubber. The leg lift will be absorbed by the upper body with the head over the belly button (center of gravity) and the pivot foot. Hands should be in the mid-torso area on a line with the chin and belly button, above, outside, or inside the knee of the lift leg. The angle and rotation of hips and shoulders are unique to each pitcher, as is the height of the lift leg. The foot, however, should be under the knee of the lift leg, never outside it, as the body moves toward home plate.

Optimal balance is achieved if the center of gravity is stabilized slightly inside the ball of the pivot foot when the knee of the lift leg reaches its maximum height. In the windup, the only reason a pitcher steps back is to free the pivot foot for its placement in front of the rubber. Any excessive movement behind the rubber can make balance more difficult to achieve.

"TALL AND FALL"

Extremity movements (arms and legs) stop briefly at the apex of the lift leg because the knee changes direction from up to down. The total body, however, initiates movement and continues forward, toward home plate. It's at this point where pitchers have maximized potential internal energy and are ready to turn it into kinetic energy with a stride down the mound. (See figure 1.1.)

In the introduction, I discussed absorbing, directing, and delivering energy from feet to throwing middle finger and out into baseball, sequentially loading muscle and kinetic energy links. Successful, healthy pitchers at any age level load and deliver energy with dynamic balance. They must learn it in preparation to be consistent in competition.

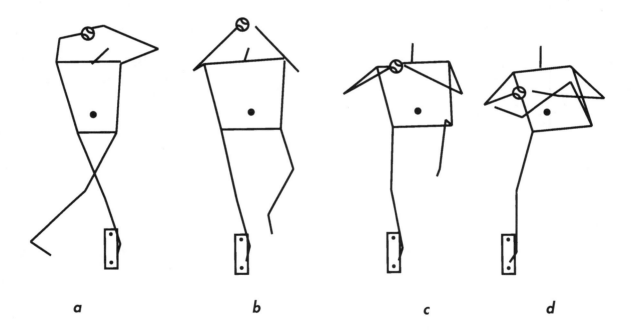

a   b   c   d

◆ **Figure 1.1, *a–d***   *Movement starts by freeing the pivot foot (a) for its placement in front of the rubber (b). Stretch movement starts with head over the center of gravity, over the ball of the pivot foot. Lift foot under lift knee (c). Dynamic balance is maintained as total body moves head over center of gravity inside ball of pivot foot (d). Lift knee reaches apex with arms, glove, and ball in front of and on line with head and center of gravity.*

LEARNING DYNAMIC BALANCE

In learning dynamic balance, pitchers should fully comprehend the logic of action and reaction. They should learn to feel what it is to collect energy around their center of gravity. I recommend working on flat ground and starting instruction with the head and feet relationship. A pitcher's head should never come off the imaginary vertical line from his pivot foot. In fact, the only time the head should ever be behind the rubber is when the pitcher is picking up the rosin bag. Arms and hands, and legs and feet should stabilize as close to the trunk as possible around a vertical post, or posture created by the head, the center of gravity, and the ball of the pivot foot. The younger the pitcher (because of strength and coordination), the less movement the better.

With the windup, keep the glove in front of the chest, hiding hand and ball, both feet over and in front of the rubber; take a small step back, or to the side, to free the pivot foot to step down in front of the rubber, making sure the heel is higher than the toes in the hole (this forces weight to the

Drills for Skills

Step Drill

Find a step or stair (even an old railroad tie will work), and assume the stretch position with posting foot on step. Flex knee, tighten abs, stride to landing foot, touch, and return. This can be done with hands fixed at chest or in a flex-T with or without light dumbbells. Keep head parallel to the ground through movement.

a   b   c

ball of the foot). Keep the head over the pivot foot at all times. Lift, don't kick, the front-side leg (use the quads, not the hips), keeping the foot under the knee to whatever height or angle is comfortable. This is a fluid, nonviolent movement, so balance shouldn't be adversely affected.

In the stretch, the pitcher's body is already set with the post foot and the landing foot perpendicular to home plate, but it is just as important to have the post foot heel higher than the toes and to have the body weight equally distributed on the balls of the feet. Hands and glove should move together and come to rest comfortably somewhere on the "elevator line" between chin and belly button and at, or just above, the highest elevation point of the lift leg knee.

A pitcher must keep his head over, on line, and slightly in front of his center of gravity (or belly button). His head must also stay between the balls or arches of his feet as he shifts body weight from back foot posting at the rubber, to front foot landing on the mound's downhill slope. After front foot landing, head and center of gravity track forward, parallel to the slope, toward the landing leg knee. When head and center of gravity have tracked forward (as far as functional strength and flexibility will allow) they become an axis of rotation for torso and arms to launch the baseball. To be dynamically balanced into delivery of a baseball, head and center of gravity continue forward, belly button to landing knee, back bending forward to a position where shoulders and head are level and as close to home plate as possible. At release point, head and center of gravity are on line with the home plate and the catcher's target. After release of the baseball, the actions of a pitcher's follow-through are inevitable, a function of what was done into foot strike and delivery of the pitch. Don't waste coaching time on how a pitcher finishes his delivery.

Understanding this chapter on dynamic balance should create an information and instruction base that sequences into the prerequisites of postural stabilization, our next absolute and the topic of our next chapter.

HOUSE RULES

Follow two basic rules to be dynamically balanced:

1. **Stay off your heels!** To be dynamically balanced, body weight must always be distributed on or between the balls of your feet.

2. **Keep your eyes level to the ground!** If your eyes are level, your head will always be over your belly button. In any human movement, if body weight is distributed on or between the balls of the feet with head over center of gravity, the person has dynamic balance.

Correct Dynamic Balance

Troy Percival twists his torso with leg lift but maintains head over center of gravity (c.g.) line inside the ball of his posting foot.

Tom Seaver lifts his knee straight up, rocks and twists his front and back shoulders, but maintains head over center of gravity (c.g.) line inside the ball of his posting foot.

Incorrect Dynamic Balance

Frank Viola arches his back with left leg and stride, losing dynamic balance because even though head is online with center of gravity (c.g.) relative to first and third base, it's behind c.g. relative to second and home plate.

Ron Guidry leans back with leg lift and stride, losing dynamic balance. Even though head is online with center of gravity (c.g.) relative to second and home plate, it's behind c.g. relative to first and third.

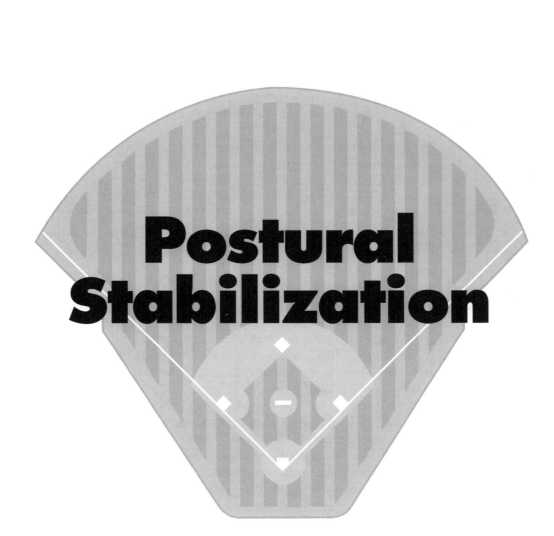

CHAPTER 2

Postural Stabilization

"Housie, you throw with your feet."
Dave Garcia, California Angels coach, 1975

"Tom, use your head, it takes care of your body."
Tatsuro Hirooka, general manager Chiba Lotte Marines, Martial Arts, 1996

Dave's statement to me during a Christmas camp brainstorming session in 1975 got all of us instructors at the San Diego School of Baseball thinking. We were trying to come up with the best way to teach youngsters to use their bodies more efficiently when throwing baseballs. What we ended up doing was to break throwing down into a sequence of teachable movements, starting with the feet. It was the first time in my baseball experience that the lower body was addressed before the upper body when it came to throwing mechanics. Hirooka's statement came literally, and figuratively, from 2,000 years of mastering movement in martial arts. It got me watching more closely what efficient throwers and pitchers did with their heads when they threw a baseball. In combination, mastering feet and head movement really simplified the instruction of pitchers.

To demonstrate the importance of this approach I continue to recommend a throwing station to precede a pitching mechanics station. We find that it makes instruction on the mound even more productive. This concept has led to the development of BioKinetics' flat-ground throwing program that I use in clinics around the world. I also use the program in rehabilitation to complement what the trainers, physical therapists, and conditioning coaches are doing off the field.

FLAT-GROUND THROWING

Garcia and Hirooka were both right. Throwing starts with the feet and then sequences through legs, torso, arms, and finally the baseball. All these movements are more efficient if the head stays firm and moves forward toward the target.

Have your players line up with partners at a throwing distance comfortable to both players. Too short always is better than too long when working on mechanics, because distance magnifies mistakes. There is also less force translated through the body on flat-ground (twice body weight vs. six times body weight on mound), so physical wear and tear is significantly less per throw (or pitch). And, once the front foot hits, neuromuscular sequencing is the same on flat or slope, so skill is taught with less stress. An athlete will never pitch properly if he can't throw properly. Start with the instruction for postural stabilization using simple flat-ground throwing and sequence skill and work toward the more complex movements of windup and stretch pitching first on flat-ground and then off the mound.

Pitchers should be encouraged to play catch on flat-ground a little differently than position players. After catching the ball from his partner, the pitcher should turn sideways and assume a stretch position. Then he should (a) initiate momentum by striding forward with front foot, (b) step behind front foot with back foot, lock in legs and hips, (c) stride forward again with front foot, break hands naturally, point glove toward

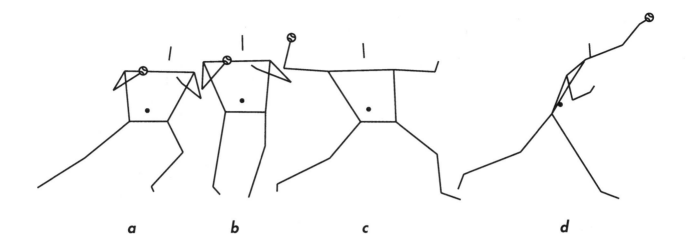

a   b   c   d

◆ Figure 2.1, *a–d*   The sequence for proper flat-ground throwing begins by having the player catch the ball and square off "ankle eye" *(a)*. The player then takes a shuffle step, using the ball-of-foot to ball-of-foot technique *(b)*. By breaking the hands, thumbs down, the player will get the elbows up into the launch position *(c)*. The final step is for the player to decelerate with the upper body out and over the landing knee *(d)*.

target, and (d) lean upper body into launch. Figure 2.1 illustrates this movement. Note how head, belly button, and feet stay parallel throughout the throw.

FLAT-GROUND PITCHING

When flat-ground pitching, master the mechanics of stretch first (fewer movable parts), then the windup. Shorten the catcher up and throw all pitches with intense mental concentration on proper form but with low physical intensity on the body and arm. Because it is low-intensity work at shorter distances, pitchers can increase the number of practice deliveries. More repetitions, with less stress, enhance the learning curve on movement skills. This is also a good way to rehabilitate a pitcher coming off an injury.

For those of you that worry about "losing stuff" by working on flat-ground at low intensity, remember: The body will never forget how to throw hard; it *will learn* how to throw wrong. Nolan Ryan seldom threw off the mound between starts in his last years with Texas. He was still throwing in the mid-90s at 44 years old because he was smart about mechanics, physical preparation, and nutrition.

PITCHING OFF A MOUND

There has been a lot of misunderstanding about a pitcher's posture and how it affects force and angle of release with fastball, breaking ball, change-up, and split finger. A pitcher must *find and keep* an upper body spine-to-hip relationship, with a *constant angle of flex* in posting knee at front leg lift, stride, and landing—directing upper body into torso rotation and launch of a baseball. All successful, healthy pitchers have minimal change in body position, up or down, right or left, or away from the catcher's target. Kinetic energy should never be misdirected or dissipated by the body, or its extremities, *away* from home plate. My "tall and fall" and Tom Seaver's "drop and drive" were incorrect when rigidly applied to every pitcher. Experience has shown both coaching methods to be a dead end, an unfortunate misinterpretation of what our eyes see in a delivery. Every pitcher postures differently, unique to his mechanical and physical implementation. In other words, he will find whatever body position is necessary to deliver the baseball, based on his structure, strength, and arm path. Start him in the wrong position and his body will usually change en route, which is inefficient. Start him in the right position and he will throw more strikes with less stress.

I have also realized that mandating stride length or stride direction is an unnecessary lesson. Why? Because with dynamic balance and postural stabilization both things happen naturally. I'm a little ahead of myself, but give this a try right now. Flex your knees, tighten your abs, lift your leg, and stride. It's virtually impossible to heel strike or toe out at landing. If you did it with intensity off a rubber going down a mound, more often than not you'd land at a distance equal to your height. It's inevitable (and easier to teach!). I will, however, discuss stride direction, since a lot of coaches still worry about throwing across the body. Striding on a straight line to home plate is secondary to the direction a pitcher achieves by just keeping head over center of gravity (c.g.) into foot strike, then rotating as late as possible (chapter 4). It's impossible for a pitcher's landing foot to hit wider than his torso. In other words, it's OK to throw

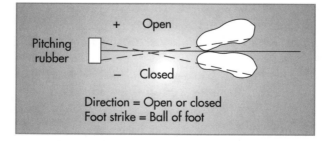

◆ Figure 2.2   When the pitcher's foot strikes the ground, it should land on the ball of the foot and can land in a slightly open, straight, or slightly closed position.

Successful, healthy pitchers, such as Roger Clemens, maintain postural stability by directing all kinetic energy towards home plate.

across your body, straight on, or slightly open, as long as you get to the ball of your foot and rotate late (see figure 2.2). Some pitchers will heel strike and roll to the ball of their foot, but most hit toe down or flat-footed. It's *not* OK to land on the heel with toe out.

I've also altered another of my past instructions: that right-handed pitchers throw from the right side of the rubber, left-handed from the left. This works for power pitchers who throw four-seam fastballs. Right-handed pitchers who throw two-seam sinkers do better from the left side of rubber; left-handed pitchers who throw two-seam sinkers do better from the right side of rubber. Why? More plate to work with. (We learned this with Kevin Brown. He kept missing down and in to right-handed hitters when he positioned himself on the third base side of the rubber. By moving to the first base side, his sinker accessed more plate and he threw more strikes!)

17

OPTIMAL PITCHING POSTURE

Watch a pitcher's head as he lifts his leg and starts a delivery toward home plate. If his head *drops* he has postured too tall. If his head *rises*, he has postured too low. If his head *leans back* (behind belly button) he has lost dynamic balance. See figure 2.3. (Leaning back is the most common posture I see with pitchers.) If his head moves *away* from home plate, he is unnecessarily misdirecting energy.

◆ Figure 2.3   Note how this pitcher leans back or arches his back to throw a baseball, thus losing dynamic balance and posture.

Drills for Skills

Towel Drill With Partner

Grip a hand towel between thumb and middle finger of the throwing hand with about 12 inches of towel showing. (This drill is calibrated around each pitcher's stride plus 12 inches of towel coming out of middle finger.) The "pitching" partner will then assume a set position with posting foot on an imaginary or real rubber, and go through a few deliveries, snapping the towel out front at release point. The "nonpitching" partner will then step off five feet from his pitcher's stride foot, big toe landing on flat ground, six feet from stride foot, big toe landing on mound. The nonpitcher partner will then face his partner, drop to a knee and present a "palm up" hand held eye high. Pitcher partner will then practice his delivery, trying to "strike" the palm up target with the hand towel. See the figures on the opposite page. Do 15 to 20 perfect deliveries and switch with partner. There is instant feedback in this towel drill because any shift of posture will result in a missed strike of the hand. With the head moving down, up, or back, the pitcher will miss short. With the head moving right or left, the pitcher will miss right or left.

(continued)

Towel Drill With Partner *(continued)*

Correct Postural Stabilization

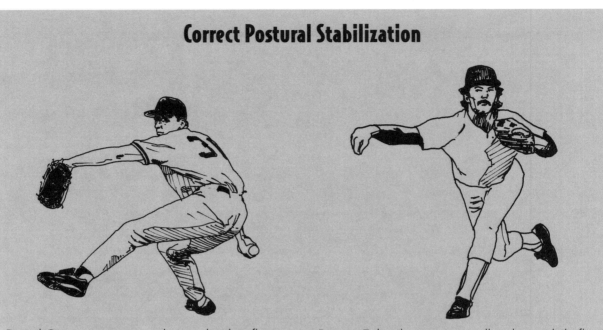

David Cone postures very low with a big flex in his posting-leg knee, but he maintains postural stabilization throughout his delivery.

Dennis Eckersley postures tall with very little flex in his posting-leg knee, but he maintains postural stabilization throughout his delivery.

Incorrect Postural Stabilization

Jose Mesa's posture changes into foot strike. His head moves left of center of gravity.

Steve Avery's torso arches as he strides forward, causing head to be behind center of gravity at foot strike.

Optimal posture for a pitcher is, in most cases, the same posture he would assume in his batting stance. To find this optimal body position, a pitcher should place feet about armpit- to shoulder-width apart, front-foot arch lined up with posting-foot big toe (a slightly closed stance.) He must have an even distribution of weight between the balls of his feet, with an equal amount of flex in both knees. Torso and head should have a slightly forward lean from hips and lower body. Each pitcher's head should remain firm and still at leg lift, stay parallel to the mound, and stay on line with home plate during stride, foot strike, torso rotation, and launch of baseball.

If his head goes down or up, the fix is more or less flex in the knees, respectively. If his head leans back, the fix is tightening abs and low back. If his head moves away from home plate, the fix is to narrow the stance and keep nose to knee at leg lift.

Remember to teach stretch delivery first, then windup. Because there are fewer movable parts, it's quicker to master.

CHAPTER 3

Flex-T Elbow Alignment at Foot Strike

"I don't know what it is I'm looking for,
but I recognize it when I see it."
Pro scout describing arm action

There has always been argument about proper arm action when pitching a baseball. Short arming, hooking, wrapping, pushing, and pie throwing are all phrases that describe a nontraditional arm path. Submarine, side arm, three-quarter, and overhand are phrases that describe arm slots at release point. Historically, pitchers who got hitters out were left alone, no matter what their arm path, or arm slot, looked like. Pitchers who didn't get hitters out, or didn't stay healthy, were subjected to countless, well-intentioned changes that most often failed. Three-dimensional motion analysis has allowed us to quantify arm and body movement externally. Electromyogram (EMG) testing and arthroscopic surgeries have allowed a peek at arm and body stresses internally. What has sports science and sports medicine taught us about arm action? Biomechanically, the longest any pitcher's arm can be is the distance from front elbow to throwing elbow at foot strike. Forearms, wrists, and hands account for style, not substance, in arm path. Quite simply, they are along for the ride until shoulders square up to home plate. If dynamic balance, postural stabilization, elbow alignment, and forearm angle into foot strike are efficient, total arm action takes care of itself! Physiologically, if arm speed (genetics) doesn't match up with arm and body strength (physical preparation), then dynamic balance, postural stabilization, elbow alignment, and forearm angle into foot strike change proportionately to the pitcher's arm speed and strength imbalance. A pitcher will create whatever contortion is necessary and stress whatever joint happens to get involved to put energy into a baseball for a strike at home plate. Strength and fatigue issues will be discussed with more detail in part II. Chapter 3 will address the biomechanics of arm position and path at front foot strike as "equal and opposite elbow alignment and forearm angle." Arms are approximately 7 percent of body weight. There must be 3.5 percent evenly distributed on both sides of the axis created by head and belly button and torso posture.

PROPER FOREARM-TO-ELBOW ANGLES

Misaligned elbows and unequal forearm angles change the body's leverage points, resulting in excess stress and inefficient release points. My instruction to get elbows up for deception was only part of the equation. It's better to teach lining the elbows up with equal forearm-to-elbow angles around dynamic balance and postural stabilization. Here's why. Just before, right at, and just after front foot contact, successful, healthy pitchers attain and maintain a 180-degree elbow-to-elbow alignment. The elbows may have a tilt, or a twist, on the horizontal or vertical plane, respectively, but they are still in a straight line with each other. We'll see in chapters 4 and 5 that (1) the elbows will hyperextend as the torso initiates rotation into launch and (2) by the time the torso and shoulders have rotated to face home plate, both elbows will be slightly flexed in front of shoulder points in what I now call the flex-T position. Look at figure 3.1. The illustration and stick figures show this straight-line relationship

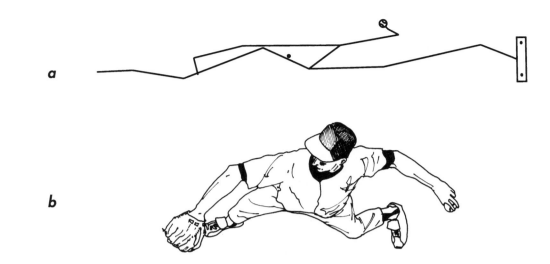

◆ **Figure 3.1, a–b**   This overhead view shows how the body lines up, creating a straight line from elbow to elbow.

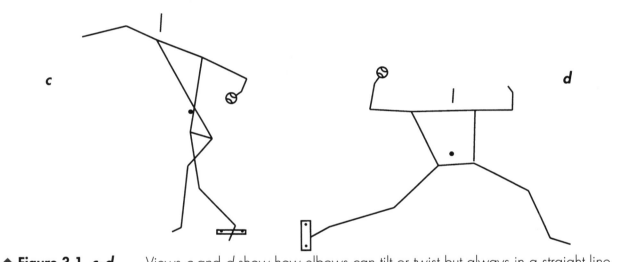

◆ **Figure 3.1, c–d**   Views c and d show how elbows can tilt or twist but always in a straight line.

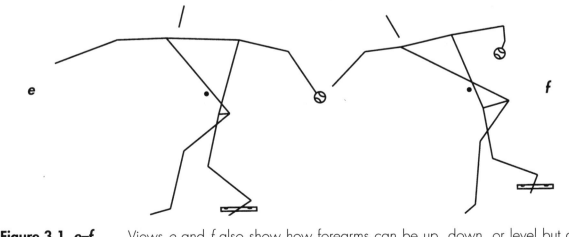

◆ **Figure 3.1, e–f**   Views e and f also show how forearms can be up, down, or level but always equal in angle.

between elbows in tilting and twisting deliveries. Note, also, that forearms can be up, down, or level, but together; elbows must be equal and opposite of one another, with the *angle* of elbow to forearm the same in both arms.

ARM ACTION DURING DELIVERY

Don't waste valuable coaching time trying to change the throwing arm. It's a dead end. Arm path and arm slot are genetic. If a pitcher were throwing rocks at rabbits in order to eat, that would be his arm action. The fix is in changing the glove side to line up with the throwing side. Identify a pitcher's natural arm action by watching him play catch and throw on flat ground, fielding grounders, line drives, fly balls, and so forth. In my experience, the quicker the feet get into weight transfer (which is what happens on flat ground), the more natural the arm action will be when throwing. Pitchers have too much time to move on the mound, and things go wrong with arms accordingly. Once the throwing arm action is identified, at foot strike adjust glove side arm to (1) line up the elbows, (2) equalize

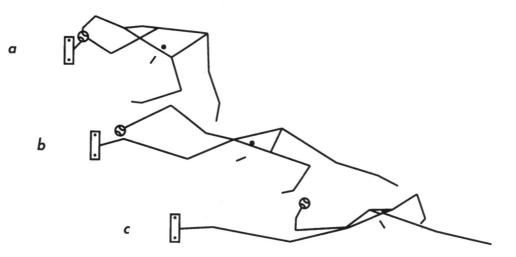

◆ **Figure 3.2, a–c**   In views a–c, this pitcher's throwing-arm path is matched with glove-arm path into foot strike.

elbow and forearm angles, (3) find a position where glove is on line or over landing foot, and (4) make sure the glove stays on line or over landing foot until baseball is released. Pitchers must fight for and keep the elbow alignment forearm angle as legs and torso decrease the distance toward home plate. Once glove and front foot achieve their maximum length, body energy and momentum is directed belly button to front knee and face to glove. Head and belly button track forward together, parallel to ground or mound, creating an axis of rotation that brings throwing arm to a *fixed* or *stationary* glove-side arm. (This is discussed in detail in chapter 5.) *Nothing* on a pitcher's body should move away from home plate. A delivery that has dynamic balance, postural stabilization, elbow alignment, and forearm angle at foot strike will accomplish this efficiently and effectively—it's inevitable. (See figure 3.2.)

The mastery of elbow alignment forearm angle at foot strike combined with dynamic balance and postural stabilization sequences to a simple but critical fourth absolute, late torso rotation, the topic of our next chapter.

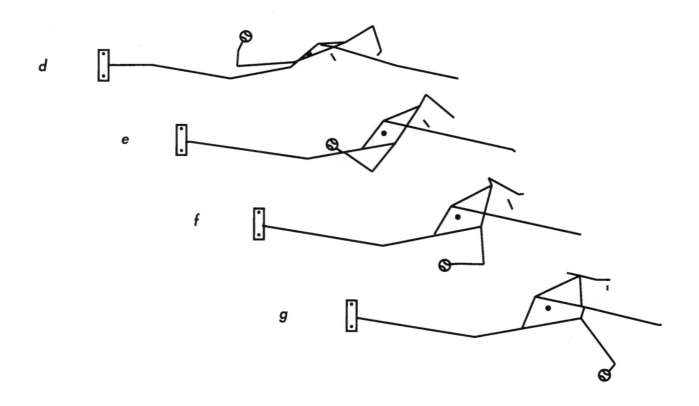

◆ **Figure 3.2, *d–g***   In views *d–g*, elbow alignment and forearm angle are equal and opposite into launch, with glove staying fixed while shoulders rotate around axis of head, center of gravity, and posture.

Elastic-Cord Drill

Secure 2-1/2 to 3 feet of light resistance elastic cord to pitcher's thumbs. Note that the pitcher's elbows should be slightly flexed, with some resistance from the cord but no restriction through range of throwing motion on a glove. Then play catch, or pitch, with a baseball. (This drill can also be done with a hand towel.) Make sure to take a "normal" arm path into foot strike and launch. The cord should resist but not restrict either arm. Misaligned elbows will drag the cord across upper body, neck, or face, depending on arm slot. Keep adjusting front-side elbow and forearm until the cord completely misses the body with each throw, pitch, or towel. In other words, stretch the cord into proper elbow forearm alignment, then deliver the ball or towel. This drill is cross-specific. It builds strength (with the stretching of the cord), endurance (with the throw, pitch, or towel), and mechanics (with the reinforcement of elbow forearm alignment and angle, respectively).

a   *b*   *c*

Correct Elbow Alignment and Forearm Angle

This angle reveals Dave Stewart's optimal elbow alignment and forearm angle at foot strike. The throwing arm/glove arm relationship is classic.

Rick Sutcliffe was very unorthodox to the eye but perfect by the computer. It's a great illustration of equal and and opposite in a nontraditional delivery.

Incorrect Elbow Alignment and Forearm Angle

Pedro Astacio's inefficient elbow alignment may account for his recent injuries and inconsistent performance.

Joey Hamilton has a great throwing arm, but his glove arm really misaligns into launch.

CHAPTER 4

Late Torso Rotation

"He's sneaky fast,"
"His fastball is harder than it looks,"
"I can't pick up his pitches. . . ."
Hitters describing Greg Maddux

This is a short chapter but very long on its importance to delivery. I've mentioned that late torso rotation is a simple concept but a difficult mastery for coach and pitcher. Why? Because it requires neuromuscular patience, and most pitchers are just plain in a hurry to throw a baseball. Obviously, when pitchers are rushing, flying out, or spinning off (actions that drive pitching coaches crazy!) their bodies are working out of sequence with the kinetic energy that's coming from the feet after their weight transfer. Think of it this way: When absorbing, directing, and delivering energy, remember that feet deliver legs, legs deliver torso, torso delivers arms, and arms deliver baseball. Any physical action from a body part that occurs out of this chain of neuromuscular energy will inhibit strikes and increase stress. Late torso rotation explains why some pitchers with great fastballs get rocked and why some pitchers with seemingly marginal stuff get people out. It's a teachable part of skill in both windup and stretch deliveries with just a basic understanding of the required movement. This chapter should provide coach and pitcher with better solutions for what has been one of pitching's longest running performance and health problems.

When pitchers shift their weight from ball of foot to ball of foot they are biomechanically and physically more efficient if they rotate their torso (with dynamic balance, postural stabilization, and elbow alignment forearm angle) as late as possible. Laws of physics dictate that the longer (in time) and farther (in distance) mass moves, the more momentum is created. The more feet, legs, and torso (which are 93 percent of body weight) work to create force and energy, the less the *arms* (at 7 percent of body weight) will have to work to deliver that force and energy. A consistent release point is achieved with less shoulder and elbow joint trauma—more strikes, less stress, hallelujah! There are secondary benefits: (1) the ball travels less distance; one foot of distance is equivalent to 3 mph with a hitter's perception of velocity); and (2) the ball's movement occurs closer to home plate. (Drag crisis, or seams interacting with air resistance, happens later, causing the ball to move later and impeding a hitter's read of fastball, curveball, change-up, or split finger.)

A way to quantify late torso rotation is to measure the distance a pitcher's posting foot has moved from the rubber at release point. This distance will be at least one-quarter of stride length if dynamic balance, postural stabilization, and elbow alignment forearm angle lead into a late axis of rotation. (See figure 4.1.)

Another way to verify late rotation is to perform the towel drill (see chapter 2). Premature rotation will cause the pitcher to miss on line and short of striking zone. Late rotation results in towel strike every time.

You now have information and instruction on technique for four pitching absolutes: (1) dynamic balance, (2) postural stabilization, (3) elbow alignment forearm angle at foot strike, and (4) late torso rotation. If you can grasp the concepts and the logic of these applications, if you can

HOUSE RULES

There's really only one rule for this absolute: Successful, healthy pitchers initiate an upper-body axis of rotation at about 75 percent of their stride length. In other words, with good pitchers, their axis, or the line of head over belly button (center of gravity), gets to about three-quarters of whatever stride length they attain *before* torso and shoulders begin rotating aligned elbows, angled forearms, glove, and baseball into launch. Most of the marquee pitchers in the major leagues rotate even later. For example, motion analysis at BioKinetics reveals that Greg Maddux has an axis of rotation at 83 percent of his stride length. How stress-free and full of strikes is Greg? No missed starts in nine-plus years, less than one walk per nine innings, a sneaky fastball with late movement on all pitches, and four Cy Young Awards (ho-hum!).

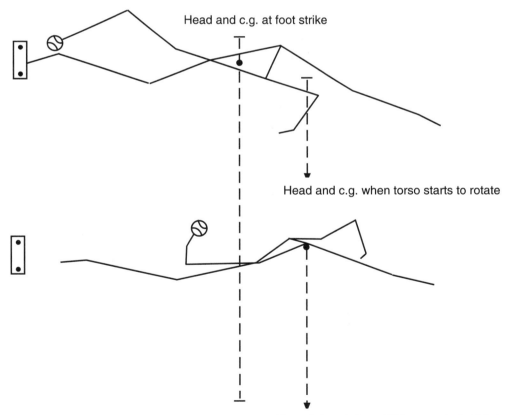

Head and c.g. at foot strike

Head and c.g. when torso starts to rotate

Torso into rotation at 75 percent of stride length

inform and instruct technique in this sequence, then absolute 5, flex-T elbow position at release point, the subject of the final chapter of part I, will flow just like the kinetic links in a pitcher's delivery!

◆ **Figure 4.1**   The posting foot will leave the rubber by a distance at least one-quarter of the stride length if a pitcher has late torso rotation at the release point.

"Get By Me" Drill

On flat ground or mound, have a coach or another player stand with (a) exactly the same posture as the pitcher and (b) lead foot at the same distance but one foot off the line created between the posting foot and the landing foot of the pitcher at maximum stride length. Then have a pitcher throw a baseball, or shadow a towel, *without touching* the coach or other player throughout delivery. This cannot be accomplished with premature rotation. Some body part, usually elbow, forearm, or glove, will contact the "get by me" guy. If the pitcher goes past the "get by me" guy in a delivery without touching him, then he's learned to rotate late!

Correct Torso Rotation

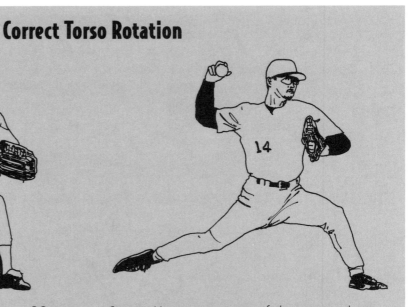

Greg Maddux's axis of rotation is at 83 percent of stride length, and his torso is just starting to rotate into launch.

Satoru Komiyama, one of the top pitchers in Japan, takes his axis of rotation to about 80 percent of stride length.

Incorrect Torso Rotation

Steve Avery's axis of rotation is at about 60 percent of stride length and starts before front foot contact.

Joey Hamilton's axis of rotation is a little less than 60 percent of stride length and starts before front contact.

CHAPTER 5

Flex-T Elbow Position at Release Point

"No one pitch, thrown properly,
puts any more stress on the arm than any other pitch."
Alan Blitzblau, Biomechanist

When I first heard Alan Blitzblau's remark on the previous page, I was more than a little skeptical. He had to be wrong. For many years, I, like everyone else, had been telling parents of Little Leaguers that their youngsters should not throw curveballs, that curveballs were bad for a young arm. "Now wait a minute," I said, "you've just discounted what's been taught to young pitchers all over the United States. Are you sure?" "I'm sure," he responded. Alan sat down in front of the computer and showed me what he had discovered. From foot to throwing elbow, every pitch has exactly the same neuromuscular sequencing. The only body segments that change when a different type of pitch is thrown are the forearm, wrist, hand, and fingers, and they change only in angle. Arm speed is the same, the arm's external rotation into launch is the same, and pronation during deceleration is the same. It is the different angles of the forearm, wrist, hand, and fingers that alter velocity, rotation, and flight of a ball.

He also revealed another surprise. The grip of a pitch is secondary to this angle, and all pitches leave the middle finger last! This was blasphemy. I was stunned. But Alan wasn't finished. "Tom, for every one-eighth inch the middle finger misses the release point when the arm snaps straight at launch, it (the ball) is eight inches off location at home plate So throwing strikes means getting the middle finger to a quarter-sized spot on the middle of the baseball with every pitch." Wow!

This chapter will dispel myths about what happens to pitcher's elbows, forearms, wrists, and fingers at release point. For years, pitching coaches (me included) taught pitchers to "pull" their glove-side elbow to their hip when throwing. We all thought this was a power movement that would increase arm speed and velocity. For years, pitching coaches (me included) taught pitchers to loosen grips for "wrist snap," "off center" the ball for movement, and separate hands "thinking fastball on all pitches," finding and delivering off-speed or breaking ball pitches while the arm was en route. We all taught incorrectly; what our eyes saw wasn't what pitchers actually did!

By chance during the off-season in 1996, I asked Dan Moffet, our current computer whiz at BioKinetics, to quantify the elbow positions of a few pitchers at foot strike (chapter 3) and release point. I was preparing for a presentation at the 1997 ABCA Convention in Dallas, Texas, and wanted some valid numbers. What he got from the three-dimensional data (table 5.1) was quite a surprise.

The angles and distances of elbows, forearms, wrists, thumbs, and middle fingers at release point showed quite the opposite of what we had been instructing. Successful, healthy pitchers kept *both* elbows in front of head and center of gravity (c.g.) line when delivering a baseball. In fact, the more out front and the more fixed glove-side elbow positioning was, the better the pitcher seemed to be. With forearms, wrists, thumbs, and middle fingers, successful, healthy pitchers had

- established fastball, breaking ball, off-speed forearms, and wrist angle at *separation;*
- held their wrists *perfectly straight* at release point on all pitches; and

- placed their middle fingers on *middle of baseball* at release point with all pitches (except the split finger in which their *thumb* found middle of baseball.

If you are at all like I was, at this point you are thinking "Oh my! How many kids have I misinformed?" Well, don't look back, look to change and move forward. Here's the information and instruction.

Table 5.1

PITCHING ELBOW QUANTITATIVE ANALYSIS

The following measurements are elbow angles and locations at front foot landing and torso rotation into release point.

Nolan Ryan—Elbows are 195 degrees (hyperextension) at foot strike. Front elbow is 10 inches in front of center of gravity (c.g.) during torso rotation into release point.

Todd Van Poppel—Elbows are 226 degrees (hyperextension) at foot strike. Front elbow is 8.66 inches in front of c.g. during torso rotation into release point.

Roger Clemens—Elbows are 185 degrees (hyperextension) at foot strike. Front elbow is 11.17 inches in front of c.g. during torso rotation into release point.

Orel Hersheiser—Elbows are 190 degrees (hyperextension) at foot strike. Front elbow is 7.82 inches in front of c.g. during torso rotation into release point.

Kevin Brown—Elbows are 193 degrees (hyperextension) at foot strike. Front elbow is 13.58 inches in front of c.g. during torso rotation into release point.

Cade Gaspar—Elbows are 183 degrees (hyperextension) at foot strike. Front elbow is 5.05 inches in front of c.g. during torso rotation into release point.

Rob Nen '89—Elbows are 205 degrees (hyperextension) at foot strike. Front elbow is 12 inches in front of c.g. during torso rotation into release point.

Rob Nen '94—Elbows are 187 degrees (hyperextension) at foot strike. Front elbow is 13.97 inches in front of c.g. during torso rotation into release point.

ENERGY TRANSLATION AT LAUNCH

The more in front and the more *fixed* front elbow position is at launch, the stronger a pitcher will be with all pitches (see figure 5.1.) He'll also be more efficient in sequential muscle loading and better able to find a consistent release point. As energy is translated from feet to middle finger of the throwing hand, a *fixed* front elbow *directs* all force and power into the throwing arm. If the front elbow moves, even with perfect timing, energy is split and misdirected *away* from home plate. Visualize a Y; energy comes up the base to where the Y splits. If both sides move then energy is split. If the front side stays firm, then all energy goes to the throwing side. With a moving front side, kinetic muscle links fire out of sequence, causing the arm to be *pulled* or *dragged* by the torso through its natural genetic path. This places excess strain on the shoulder and elbow, creating an inconsistent elbow-to-elbow relationship and a widening cone of release that should actually be narrowing. To get a proper feel for this process, sit in a pec deck machine with resistance set at 50 pounds. (That's about what a 90 mph fastball puts on your arm.) Bring your glove-side arm out to a position right in front of your nose and hold the machine there. Slowly start your throwing arm forward and at the same time let your glove-side arm come back. Feel the stress on throwing shoulders and elbow. Go back to the original position. Start the throwing arm forward but keep glove-side arm locked in front of your nose. Notice there is significantly less stress on the throwing arm. That is what's supposed to happen. Also a wide cone of release adversely affects both the angle and the distance of the baseball in its flight to the plate. So, besides excess shoulder and elbow stress and inconsistent release point, hitters will actually see all pitches earlier. They will also recognize breaking ball and off-speed pitches quicker because nonpower pitches leave the middle finger with a different trajectory, being cast above the fastball plane.

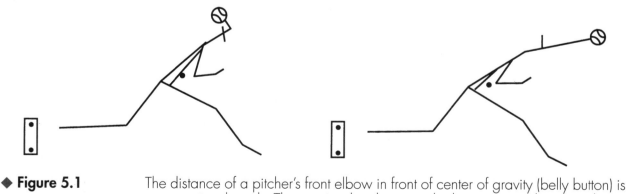

◆ **Figure 5.1**   The distance of a pitcher's front elbow in front of center of gravity (belly button) is constant into launch. The greater this distance, the less strain and more strikes.

RELEASE POINT

For the forearm, wrist, hand, thumb, and middle finger to impart maximum force or rotation on a baseball, enery must pass through the centerline of a baseball. There should be no wrist twist, wrist snap, bent wrist, or off-center finger pressure as the ball wouldn't—actually it *couldn't*—advance forward. The forearm, wrist, hand, thumb, and middle finger line up with the center of the ball, *completely* straight at the release point. This direct line from elbow to middle finger becomes an axis for straight, supinate, or pronate positioning.

Figure 5.2 shows the release position for the fastball, curveball, and screwball. In simple terms, if the palm faces the catcher, it's a fastball (see figure 5.2a). If the palm is supinate (that is, turned in toward the pitcher), it's a curveball (see figure 5.2b). If the palm is pronate, or facing away from the pitcher, it's a screwball (see figure 5.2c). Notice in all cases that the centerline of the ball rests on the thumb. What about the release position of other pitches? A split-finger fastball is still a fastball, so the angle of the wrist is the same as a fastball. The palm faces the catcher. A slider is about one half the angle of a curveball—the palm is not quite facing the pitcher but is angled a bit more toward the catcher. Going the other way (pronate), a sinker is about one-half the angle of the screwball—the palm doesn't face straight out but is angled a bit more toward home plate. With the fastball, breaking ball, and change-up, the middle of the the baseball must leave the middle finger last because it's the longest finger on the hand. With the split finger, the thumb imparts the power and rotation.

BASIC GRIPS

The following section illustrates the basic grips and finger placement on the baseball. But remember, a batter doesn't hit what a pitcher throws; he hits what he sees. Changing speeds and having late movement and good location make it difficult for hitters to see and read a pitch. This can be taught to pitchers of any age, and is explained in detail in table 5.2 on pitch velocity on page 46. Remember that the key to a pitch's movement is not the grip—it is arm speed with proper forearm, wrist, and hand angle.

Fastball

There are three main grips for throwing the fastball. Throwing across four seams is a power pitcher's fastball grip. Biomechanically, it maximizes force through the center axis of the ball and imparts a reverse spin on the ball that works in the airflow to minimize the pull of gravity. The ball appears to hop. Actually, it drops less than the other types of fastballs.

◆ **Figure 5.2 a**   **Fastball release.** The palm faces the catcher at the fastball release point. Though the fastball can be thrown with a number of different grips, the release angle is the same. The split-finger release is in the same position, but the thumbs imparts the force, power, and rotation.

b   **Curveball release.** The palm supinates and turns in toward the pitcher at the curveball release. The slider, another breaking ball, has a similar release angle, about one-half that of the curveball.

c   **Screwball release.** The palm pronates and turns out away from the pitcher at the screwball release. The sinker also has a pronated angle of release, about one-half that of the screwball.

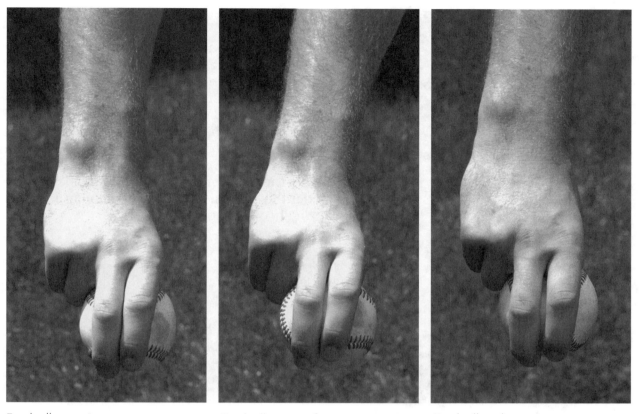

Fastball across two seams.   Fastball across four seams.   Fastball with two seams.

Throwing across two seams is a transitional grip leading to throwing with two seams. Both of these grips are for location pitchers who want to run or sink on the ball. The middle finger will impart rotation that works with gravity in the airflow to get movement horizontally or down. At the release point the arm should snap straight to full extension, with the wrist firm behind the ball and the middle finger imparting force through the center axis of the baseball.

GLOVE POSITIONING

After lining up elbows at foot strike, keep glove over the landing foot as much as possible as body rotates around head/c.g. axis to direct and deliver energy into the baseball toward the plate. Bring throwing arm elbow to a fixed glove-side elbow. Keep it firm and out front at whatever height comes natural.

Pre-set forearm, wrist, hand, and grip angles on all pitches in the glove during skill work, at separation during competition.

Split Finger

The split finger is thrown exactly like the fastball. The wrist will want to follow the middle finger off to the side. Don't let it happen. Have the pitcher pretend there is a phantom middle finger through the center of the ball. This will firm up the wrist and create the same biomechanical delivery of a regular fastball. At the release point, the arm should snap straight to full extension with the wrist firm behind the ball. The index and middle fingers should be on the side of the ball. For direction, the thumb drags on a seam under the ball which will add a tumbling action to the ball, usually off-speed.

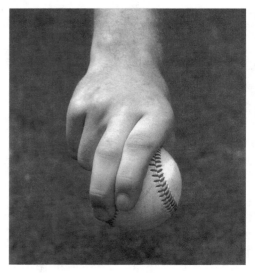

Sinker

The sinker is thrown with fastball arm speed, and with the forearm, wrist, and hand angle at one-half of full pronation. The middle finger will push through the center axis of the ball creating rotation equal to the angle of the forearm. The wrist and hand perform an inside-out action. At the release point, the arm should snap straight to full extension with the wrist firm and angled with a slight supination. This enables the middle finger to impart a push-like rotation through the center axis of the ball. A sinker is considered a velocity pitch.

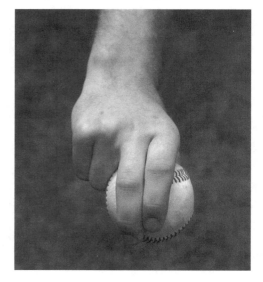

Slider

The slider is thrown with fastball arm speed. The forearm, wrist, and hand angle should be half of a karate chop. The middle finger will cut through the center axis of the ball creating rotation equal to the angle of forearm, wrist, and hand. Think of it as an outside-in action. At the release point, the arm should snap straight to full extension, with the wrist firm and angled with a slight supination. This enables the middle finger to impart a cutting rotation through the center of the ball. A slider is considered a velocity pitch.

Screwball

The "scroogie" is thrown with fastball arm speed, and the forearm, wrist, and hand angle are at full pronation, leading with the thumb; this enables the middle finger to impart rotation over the center axis of the ball, creating a spin that works with gravity in an inside-down action. At the release point, the arm should snap straight to full extension with the wrist firm and angled palm out. This enables the middle finger to impart a maximum of pronated rotation on the ball. A screwball is considered an off-speed pitch because the arm angle puts rotation, not force, on the ball.

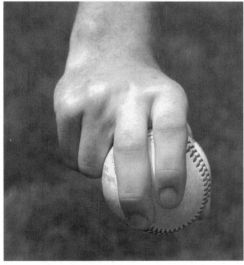

Curveball

The curve is thrown with fastball arm speed, and with forearm, wrist, and hand angle at full supination, karate chop-like. This enables the middle finger to impart rotation over the center axis of the ball, creating a spin that works with gravity in an outside-down action. At the release point, the arm should snap straight to full extension again, with the wrist firm and angled in a full karate chop. This enables the middle finger to impart a maximum of supinated rotation on the ball. A curveball is considered an off-speed pitch because the arm puts rotation, not force, on the ball.

Circle Change

The circle change is the same as a screwball, but the O should be thrown directly at the catcher.

Choke all pitches. Squeeze thumb and middle finger on fastball, breaking ball, change-up; squeeze thumb only on split finger. This helps to eliminate floppy wrist with weak or tired pitchers (from Little League to major league.)

Well, now you have the fifth and final of contemporary sport science's pitching absolutes—flex-T elbow, forearm, wrist, thumb, and middle finger position at release point. Learn them and let the inevitable happen!

Table 5.2

PITCH VELOCITY

Speed ranges for the types of pitches (fastball, slider, curveball, and change-up) at different levels of play are unique to each pitcher—a function of his best fastball. At any level, hitters don't hit what a pitcher is throwing; they hit what they see. It's great to have a 90 mph fastball, but a pitcher doesn't have to throw hard to get hitters out. Pitchers get hitters out with location, movement, and change of speed.

It's arm speed that makes a baseball go fast, and arm speed, like foot speed, is genetic. Good mechanics and proper conditioning won't improve velocity; they'll only help make velocity consistent. So what can a pitcher do to improve the effectiveness of his fastball? He can master different pitches; and different speeds with these pitches. This will make it more difficult for hitters to see, read, and commit to swinging at what is being thrown.

Perception is reduced when various pitches are delivered with fastball arm speed without being fastballs. Here are the optimal velocity ranges for change-ups, curveballs, and sliders based on a pitcher's own best fastball (no matter what his age or natural ability).

Best fastball to best change-up = 17–20 mph slower

Best fastball to best curveball = 13–16 mph slower

Best fastball to best slider = 9–12 mph slower

These calibrations differ slightly for pitchers who throw very hard and for pitchers who throw very slow. Very hard throwers require less change of speed. Nolan Ryan's change-up (at 84 mph) was 2 mph quicker than my best fastball (at 82 mph.) Soft throwers require larger changes in the velocity of *all* their pitches. Tewksbury throws a 55 mph curveball to complement his 80 mph fastball! My screwball was 60 and it helped my fastball *look* faster than it was.

Front-Side Facilitator

The best drill I've found to improve direction, distance, and integrity of glove-side elbow is a *front-side facilitator*. It's actually two to four pounds of aerobic wrist weights held in the pitcher's glove during a throw or pitch. After lining elbows up into foot strike, the glove weight is directed toward target, firming up and stopping over landing foot. The body then glides forward and rotates to the glove weight, throwing arm closing into a narrow cone of release with glove arm. Done correctly the pitcher will feel little, if any, resistance from the glove weight. Done incorrectly, the glove weight will misdirect force and energy proportionate to the speed and distance it moves offline with target. Two to 4 pounds feel like 10 to 20 pounds on glove-side shoulder and arm! The front-side facilitator can be used with the towel drill also.

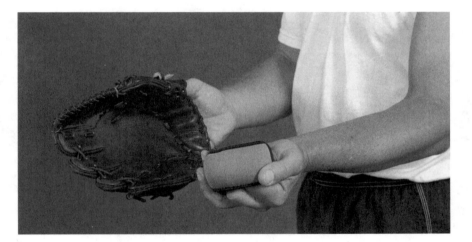

The front-side facilitator drill with weight to be placed into glove. If the glove is offline, the weight will misdirect energy and feel noticably heavy. Done correctly, with glove in proper alignment with the target, it should feel like an empty glove.

Hockey Puck Drill

The best drill I've found for reinforcing forearm, wrist, hand, and grip positioning into release point is the *hockey puck drill*. Get a hockey puck, stand about 15 feet from a concrete or brick wall in the stretch position, pre-set fastball, breaking ball, change-up, or split finger, and with low intensity throw the hockey puck against the wall. If mechanics are efficient the hockey puck will bounce off the wall and roll, tirelike, straight back to pitcher. If anything in the pitcher's mechanics is out of alignment into release point, the hockey puck won't bounce or roll straight back.

(continued)

Hockey Puck Drill *(continued)*

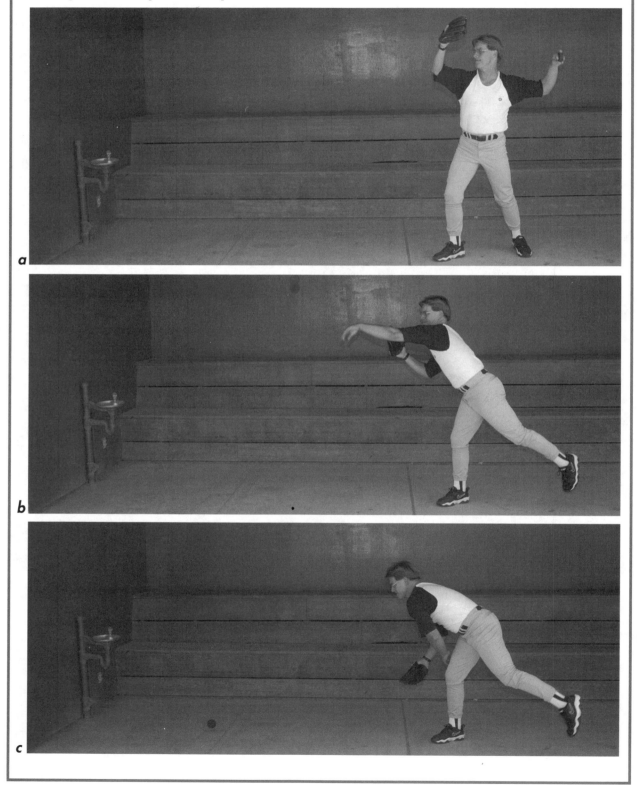

Two Knee Drill

The best drill I've found to integrate throwing and pitching release points at any distance (to tolerance) is the *two knee drill*. On flat ground, square off to your target, knees shoulder width apart. Lean forward until you feel like you may fall and tighten your abdominals and lower back to maintain that posture. With this body position, match your normal arm path with an equal and opposite glove side and rotate your torso into launch. With short, medium, and long tosses from this position, the smallest posture change or inefficient glove movement will cause the throw to miss right or left or up or down, respectively. Done properly, even Little Leaguers can throw a baseball accurately at 60 to 75 feet. Work up to 10-15 perfect tosses at 120 feet (no matter what your age or skill level). It's the longest throw you'll have to make in competition!

With pitching, you can use a baseball or a hockey puck, with or without a front-side facilitator. Set up with a partner 30 to 45 feet away, pre-set (in the glove) all your grips with proper forearm, wrist, and hand angle. Throw 10 to 15 perfect pitches each with your fastball, breaking ball, and change-up or split-finger.

Correct Position at Release Point

Randy Johnson's glove is over stride foot at landing and stays there as body and throwing arm glide forward and rotate into a firm front side elbow. The glove has not moved at release point.

Incorrect Position at Release Point

Jose Rijo's glove is at center of gravity (c.g.) and his elbow is behind c.g. The result isn't stuff or command; it's arm stress and injury.

Ditto with Dave Righetti. His glove is at c.g., not over stride foot.

Drills for Skills

One-Hop Drill

The simplest release-point drill I've found for getting a pitcher "out front" is the *one-hop drill*. On flat ground or mound, move home plate to about 45 feet and one hop *all pitches* off the plate into a catch screen. A pitcher cannot bounce a pitch off the shortened plate unless his release point is out front. (Front-side facilitator can also be used in this one-hop drill, and remember to pre-set all pitches!)

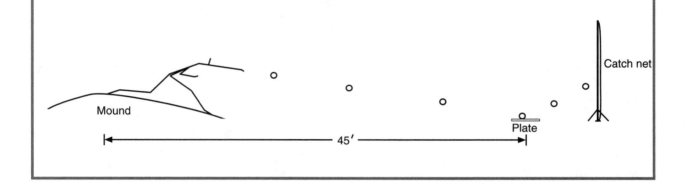

Mound

Catch net

Plate

45'

PART II

FUNCTIONAL PHYSICAL TRAINING

"Pitchers seldom break down in big muscles; injury problems usually occur in smaller muscles or connective tissues, and stronger doesn't necessarily mean faster."

Wherever I go in the world, pitchers ask me if weight training will help them throw harder. They want to know if bigger is better, they want to know what muscles to build, and they want to know when to build them. Coaches, however, want to know if weight training will keep their pitchers healthy. And, if so, what type of weight training is best: free weights or machines, lift light or lift heavy? There are a lot of baseball training misconceptions out there, and this part of *The Pitching Edge* is written to identify and explain a few of the critical ones. Think of chapters 7 and 9 as Cliff notes—a complement to my book *Fit to Pitch* that provides in-depth training protocols for preseason, in-season, and postseason preparation. Probably the biggest misconception with pitchers and their fastballs is that an athlete will throw harder if he lifts weights. In reality, arm speed and arm strength and endurance are two different things. Arm speed is genetic. Training arm strength and endurance will only support the fast-twitch muscle tissue with which a pitcher was born. A pitcher does not have to be strong to throw hard; he must, however, have enough *functional* strength to support the sequential muscle loading that gets kinetic energy from feet to middle fingertip and out into baseball. With increased throwing workloads, a pitcher is only as strong as his weakest link.

When I first started coaching and consulting in the Pacific Rim, I was amazed at the number of pitches their athletes could throw without breaking down. I saw Japanese, Taiwanese, and Korean hurlers work up to 800 pitches per week with no complaints and no ill effects. They weren't built like Superman, and their mechanics were nothing special. Then I'd return to the United States and watch our athletes come up with sore shoulders and elbows, throwing 250 to 300 pitches per week. And these kids were bigger athletes with pretty good mechanics, on regular strength programs, and with conservative throwing workloads! There had to be an explanation. Those of you that have followed my research, books, and videos know I believe in an integration of mechanics, strength, and pitch totals. You also know I started preaching resistance training to coaches and pitchers 25 years ago. In part II of this book (and in my book *Fit to Pitch*) I'm revising the sermon to explain what we've learned when comparing the training protocols from both sides of the Pacific. Basically (1) absolute strength in baseball isn't as important as functional strength; (2) muscle strength must be complemented by muscle endurance and joint integrity; (3) cardiopulmonary stamina must balance aerobic and anaerobic capacity; and (4) with increased throwing workloads no pitcher will be healthy enough to deliver strikes consistently unless he integrates all of the above in a year-round fitness program. It's actually a combination of Pacific Rim and U.S. training protocols, the best of the baseball worlds!

What is this fitness program? It's *functional cross-training* with six components: (1) flexibility work, (2) bodywork, (3) joint-integrity work, (4) machine work, (5) free-weight work, and (6) aerobic/anaerobic work. (See figure II.1.) The concept of combining skill training and resistance training is where the term *cross-training* came from. The term *functional cross-training* came from identifying efficiencies of movement to pitch a baseball and then creating physical conditioning protocols to support repetition of that movement. A pitcher can't build arm strength by just throwing, because throwing is a tearing-down process. He must build arm strength with resistance training. Arm endurance is built with some combination of throwing, resistance training, and aerobic/anaerobic training. Arm strength training and arm endurance training must be coordinated around pitch totals.

Basically, pitchers prepare to pitch, they pitch, and then they work to repair the effects of pitching. A pitcher's job description (reliever or starter) may alter his program emphasis *within* training protocols (see *Fit to Pitch* for a pitch total quantification with frequency or duration of appearance), but functional cross-training protocols must be consistently followed if coach and player want to maximize performance and minimize risk of injury. Physical conditioning for a pitcher is a function of balanced muscle strength, flexibility, and muscular endurance; optimal stamina or cardiorespiratory efficiency; and proper nutritional intake. Sound like a lot? It is, because preparing to pitch requires the interaction of these variables in a yearly cycle of building, tapering, and maintaining. The strength variable, the maximizing of power with flexibility, is illustrated in figure II.1.

The competitive season and maintenance training is one of four macrocycles that make up a baseball pitcher's year. It is the longest cycle and is made up of microcycles, with submaximal lifting in the intervals between game appearances. I use the following analogy in my clinics and lectures: A professional pitcher's competitive season is like an ultramarathon made up of a number of individual races and sprints of

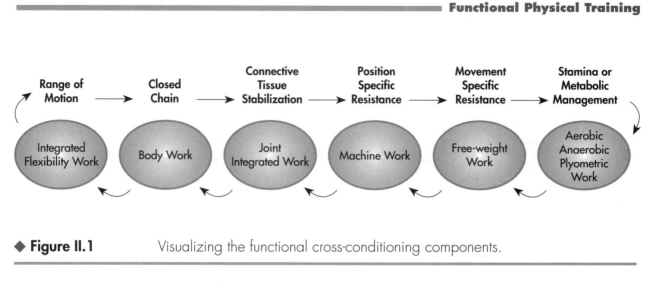

◆ **Figure II.1**   Visualizing the functional cross-conditioning components.

various distances. Starting pitchers will work the equivalent of 30 to 35 10-kilometer runs, relievers as many as 80 quarter-mile sprints. But all pitchers benefit from a properly designed year-round training program tailored to fit the individual job description, motivation, mechanical efficiency, and genetic makeup. A breakdown of yearly macrocycles and when actual throwing occurs appears in figure II.2.

Skill is neuromuscle memory. Skill training and resistance training protocols should complement each other. Nerves don't work in fat; they work best in lean muscle tissue. A combination of movement-specific anaerobic, sustained aerobic, and low-impact plyometric activity is the best way to burn unnecessary body fat. Also, it is important to know that just lifting weights won't burn body fat. I recommend 30 to 45 minutes of jogging, biking, stationary biking, or pool work (swimming, treading water, running in the shallow end) at least three times a week (more if there is a weight problem). It's actually metabolic management, and the effects are all positive. It gets oxygen to the muscle tissue more efficiently; this means the muscles work better and longer in competition. It also increases blood flow to muscle tissues; this means the wastes of muscle fatigue and muscle failure (lactic acid) are flushed out more efficiently. Metabolic fitness means that critical nutrients are brought to stressed muscles for quicker

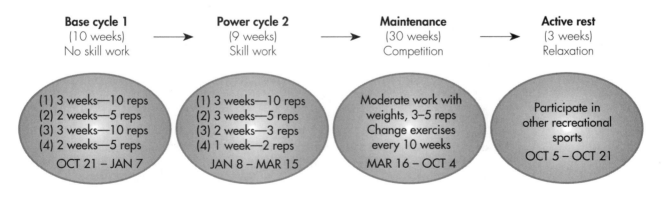

◆ **Figure II.2**   A yearly training schedule for pitchers.

healing to speed up recovery time between outings. I call it "changing your oil," and I make all my consults do stamina work—both starters and relievers. The stamina side of the conditioning process is illustrated in figure II.3.

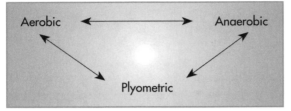

◆ **Figure II.3**   Aerobic exercise should be performed three times per week for 30 to 45 minutes each time (minimum) for all cycles. Anaerobic exercise should be done three to five times per week during the base, power, and maintenance cycles. Plyometric exercises can be performed daily, to tolerance, in both aerobic and anaerobic training.

COMMITMENT AND CONSISTENCY

Training takes commitment and consistency. There is no reason for pitchers of any age and at any competitive level to ignore the benefits of being physically prepared. It maximizes their chances of succeeding and minimizes their risk of injury. I don't deny that it is possible to be a very skilled and successful pitcher without being in shape. However, at some point in every pitcher's career, his body will be taxed beyond what skill alone can support. That is what a coach must sell to the player. The logic is inescapable. It is in the practical application where pitchers get into mental and physical denial because training is hard work. However, getting into top physical shape is the hardest part. Once an optimal conditioning level has been reached, we will see that it is possible to maintain that level (indefinitely) at about 70 percent of base.

A short story about Nolan Ryan might get your "motivation muscle" activated. The Rangers were in Cleveland for a weekend series with the Indians. This was two years before the new stadium was built. Nolan (who was scheduled to pitch Saturday night) and I visited a downtown health club on Friday morning for a workout. When we asked about lifting weights on Sunday (Nolan always lifts the day after he pitches), the manager of the club said that it was closed on Sunday (I think the whole city of Cleveland closed on Sunday). Nolan then asked in his slow Texas drawl, "Is there anything y'all can do to get us in here Sunday morning?" The manager replied, "Let me check." Now picture this: The club is in the basement of a zillion-story office complex in downtown Cleveland, which is closed on Sunday, but Nolan will lift Sunday, somewhere, no matter what. I know this, Nolan knows this, and before long so do building security, the building's management office, and the owner of the building itself (who we found out later had to give the final clearance.) "OK," the club manager said. "You are all set for Sunday morning. Someone will be here to let you in. What time?" "Let's see," Nolan said. "Bus leaves for the stadium at 10:30. We'll want to get some breakfast. How about 6:30 A.M.?" (His workouts are about three hours long.) "Is that all right?" "Sure thing," the manager said. "Just bang hard on the lobby door so whoever is here will hear you." Well, we won the Saturday night game, but it was a long one. I don't know about Nolan, but I got to bed about 1:30 A.M. Anyway, as I was riding down the hotel elevator at 6 A.M. on Sunday (in downtown Cleveland the sun isn't even up) to lift weights with Nolan Ryan, I thought, "What's wrong with this picture?" It occurred to me that this is motivation, dedication, consistency, and commitment all rolled into one, and it is why the big gun was still competing at age 46. By the way, the office building owner let us in to work out and stayed to lift with us. Successful people are motivated any time of the day, and that is commitment.

Remember as you read through part II that with throwing workloads, a pitcher is only as strong as his weakest link. Your goal should be learning how to train each link to support genetics and skill in competition. Programs and tools for training will be discussed in chapter 6, while chapter 7 discusses how to transer training to performance. Both chapters will synthesize the best information and instruction available in today's baseball world on the physical preparation of a pitcher.

Programs and Tools for Training

"You don't run the ball over home plate."
Johnny Sain, Atlanta Braves pitching coach, 1978

"He can bench press 325 pounds,
but he can't throw strikes."
*Anonymous player on Jack Armstrong,
Cleveland Indians pitcher, from the Texas Rangers bench, 1992*

"I work just as hard to throw hard as I always did;
it just doesn't get there as fast."
*Bert Blyleven, California Angels pitcher,
in Anaheim Stadium weight room, 1992*

The remarks on the previous page reflect common misconceptions about the relationship of physical conditioning and pitching a baseball. Pitching requires skill, the mastery of complex movements under game conditions. You don't have to be aerobically fit, you don't have to be particularly strong, and working hard doesn't necessarily mean you will throw hard.

However, an athlete properly trained and aerobically fit, who has balanced strength, neuromuscular efficiency, and proper blood chemistry, will compete longer with less chance of injury. It is the difference between a couple of good years and a career.

For example, statistically, I was a marginal major league pitcher. (Scouts would say consistently marginal.) Through trial and error, I complemented my genetic talent with an optimal fitness program to support my skill level over eight major-league seasons. In short, training cannot overcome a lack of genetic talent or take the place of skill. But a physical conditioning base can support whatever talent and skill a pitcher may have.

Old-school instructors believed lifting weights was bad for pitchers, that it made a pitcher muscle bound. Up until about 20 years ago, their thinking was correct. That's because nobody really knew how to weight train a pitcher without affecting his flexibility and range of motion.

Today, if you truly understand the feet-to-fingertip kinetic energy translation of throwing mechanics, then a properly implemented training program to increase strength and flexibility through a biomechanically efficient delivery makes good sense. By "properly," I mean tailoring a program that creates a physiological balance—right side to left side, front side to back side, concentric to eccentric, and muscle to tendon, ligament, and bone.

TRAINING SPECIFIC TO PITCHERS

The body is unique when it comes to pitching. Its first line of defense against injury is muscle, its second is tendon or ligament, and its third is bone. Pitchers with tendinitis don't have the muscle strength or muscle balance to support their mechanics or the number of pitches thrown. Bone chips or spurs reflect long-term problems with muscles, tendons, ligaments, and mechanics from whatever pitching workloads were done.

Resistance training does the opposite. Muscle density builds quickest, then tendon and ligament strength, and finally bone density. In other words, conditioning puts it in the bank and throwing takes it out. It seems stupid not to have ready reserve available through resistance training.

Resistance training for pitching is different than resistance training for any other skill. Pitching involves neuromuscular memory rather than "neurofat" memory. Nerves don't work in fat, and fat doesn't help you move. Excess stored fat requires four times the energy of moving the same amount of muscle tissue.

BUILDING MUSCLE TISSUE

Bigger isn't necessarily better. Nerves work best in dense muscle tissue where cells are about equal in size. If you bulk up, you reduce the efficiency of your nerve work.

Muscle strength builds faster than tendon, ligament, and bone strength. This must be taken into consideration with any program design for each pitcher's conditioning base, arm pathologies, and age.

Preadolescent pitchers should not lift heavy weights because their muscles will gain strength at the expense of connective tissue and actually tear themselves out of a joint. They should lift their body weight instead with push-ups, dips, pull-ups, chin-ups, and sit-ups.

In the opener to part II, I told you I was really vexed when it came to understanding why the Pacific Rim pitchers could handle such large throwing workloads without breaking down. With better information about *strength* versus *endurance,* with better information about strength and endurance *benchmarks*, and with better understanding about *when* to train, the picture got a little clearer—less vexed, more flexed! I'd like to expand training information a bit and discuss training benchmarks and training timing. A pitcher's base cycle is his *building* cycle.

BUILDING VS. MAINTENANCE

Building strength is an off-season activity in which there is task-specific throwing (football, softball, or baseball tossing on flat ground) but no skill-specific throwing (pitching off a mound.) *Maintaining* strength is an in-season activity when there is task-specific, skill-specific, and competitive throwing.

Any strength-training program will take 12 to 16 weeks to implement properly. Don't try to rush Mother Nature! It is smarter and easier to work with her in the off-season for better focus, more time, and fewer distractions. Tendon and ligament strength starts balancing muscle strength by about week 10 (with proper training protocols).

The difference between building and maintaining is training to muscle failure. Training to muscle failure will build strength *off-season*. It is maintenance training to keep a base of muscle strength *in-season*. You can't build in-season because pitching is a tearing-down process that would worsen with training to muscle failure. No matter how strong you are, you get weaker as a season progresses. Depending on mechanical efficiency, throwing workloads, and maintenance training, my years of strength testing Rangers pitchers revealed that a pitcher can lose as much as 20 percent of his preseason strength base! Logic would dictate that off-season conditioning should create a base of strength and stamina broad enough to handle throwing workloads and the accompanying loss of overall strength that comes with competition.

A good guesstimate of how much upper-body strength to build in the off-season is to determine the maximum weekly throwing workloads from in-season and match it with an equal weekly volume in weight or resistance training plus 20 percent (to compensate for strength loss). This is for the upper body only. Leg work must be factored separately into a total body resistance program.

CALCULATING TRAINING VOLUMES

The following formula approximates the volume of off-season upper-body work recommended for pitchers to throw a baseball off a mound.

$$\text{Volume of work per week} = \text{\# of pitches} \times \text{velocity}^2 \times .01 \times \frac{1}{\substack{\text{mechanical} \\ \text{efficiency} \\ \text{factor}}} \times \frac{1}{\substack{\text{strength} \\ \text{loss} \\ \text{factor}}}$$

So let's see how this works for an amateur pitcher who throws 300 pitches per week off a mound (game and skill work) at 85 mph with an 80 percent mechanical efficiency (source: BioKinetics) and a 20 percent strength loss factor. He would have the following throwing workload of volume per week, upper body, in the off-season:

$$300 \times 85^2 \times .01 \times \frac{1}{.80} \times \frac{1}{.80} \cong 34{,}000 \text{ pounds}$$

Now, substitute a professional pitcher with a 90 percent mechanical efficiency rating, and you find the following workload of volume per week, upper body, in the off-season:

$$300 \times 85^2 \times .01 \times \frac{1}{.90} \times \frac{1}{.80} \cong 30{,}000 \text{ pounds}$$

Once an off-season training volume has been established, it can be maintained by lifting in-season at 70 percent of the off-season volume (same weight and lift, less reps or same reps, less weight and lift) or, in this example, 24,000 pounds and 21,000 pounds per week for our amateur and professional pitchers, respectively. Remember, these are minimums. A pitcher can train to much larger volumes. For example, Kevin Brown's maintenance program was more than Kenny Rogers's building program, though they throw about the same number of pitches per week. Once volumes have been established, a pitcher can tailor his program to light, medium, and heavy lifting days, and lift days around throwing days.

DESIGNING A STRENGTH-TRAINING PROGRAM

It is appropriate to expand on some physiological basics and some exercise physiology protocols to maximize results when training an athlete to pitch. At Bio-Kinetics, we discovered the following:

1. Three basic muscle groups accelerate the arm in X time with contraction. Two basic muscle groups decelerate the arm in X + 2 time with elongation. Therefore, decelerators should be worked one-third more than accelerators in resistance training (whenever possible) for strength balance. (See Dr. Richard Heitsch's discussion at the end of this chapter.)

2. Whenever possible, there should be rotation of the arms through a full range of motion, especially with lighter resistance work (dumbbells and cord), because cross-specific movement in training helps proprioception for the skill of throwing.

3. There is no best way to train the body. Isotonic (free weights), isokinetic (Nautilus), and isometric (resistance with no motion) exercises all work, as do combinations of these. Other effective training includes working against body weight with push-ups, chin-ups, sit-ups, and dips (some of my Rangers pitchers did their resistance work in the pool, using hand paddles and fins to increase workloads). Weights help to better quantify training effort, but each pitcher should choose what's right for him as long as it works!

4. Resistance training will not improve speed by itself. It will, however, enable a pitcher to be more neuromuscularly consistent with his talent (his maximum, genetically predetermined arm speed) on all pitches.

Overloading, however, with underloading resistance training can improve arm speed in a program specifically designed around six, five, and four-ounce baseballs. Dr. Coop DeRene and I supported this in a research project with about 200 high school and collegiate pitchers.

The idea behind underloading is to perform the skill with an implement that is 20 percent less weight than the regular competitive implement (four ounces vs. five ounces). Throwing a four-ounce baseball offers the arm offers less resistance through the throwing motion into launch. With less resistance the arm speed will be faster. Neuromuscular interaction will remember this faster arm speed, and there will be a percentage carryover when the regulation five-ounce baseball is thrown (our research showed an overall average increase of 2.5 to 3 percent).

Now that you have a baseball view of resistance training, it becomes necessary to create some training guidelines.

TRAINING PRINCIPLES

You have read through the theory and application of an upper-body resistance program; now let's add some common sense. Athletes first warm up to loosen up, then do the work or competitive activity, and finally warm down for tomorrow's work or competitive activity. The most important factors in any exercise, work, or competitive physiology program are volume intensity, workload, duration, and frequency. It should come as no surprise that these are the same factors involved in throwing workloads (see figure 6.1).

The training program can be used as part of the loosening-up and warming-up process (by varying volume, frequency, load, intensity, and duration) if skill work or game competition is the activity of the day. If resistance training is the activity of the day, then loosen up and warm up to complement the work. The training is cross-specific!

Also, we have had a lot of success with pitchers in cool-down and recovery by combining ice therapy and aerobic work (specifically stationary bike) after throwing. They all ice their arms while they ride the bike. The logic is that ice addresses the microtears and bleeding in muscle tissue. Aerobics helps to flush the lactic acid out of fatigued muscles and promotes the healing process. Nolan Ryan conducted postgame press conferences while icing and biking in the clubhouse!

Training modality	=	Volume	×	Intensity	×	Workload	×	Duration	×	Frequency
Pitching		Total work during microcycle		Practice vs. game		Per practice session per inning		Work per outing		Number of outings
Lifting		Total weight lifted during microcycle		Time between lifts		Per lift per set		Work per session		Number of sessions
Pitching and lifting		Starter = Duration ↑ more Frequency ↓ less								
		Reliever = Duration ↓ less Frequency ↑ more								
Lifting		A starter will have one or two submaximal sessions between each start. A reliever will have five to seven minisessions per week. Both starters and relievers will match up total pitching volumes with total lifting volumes.								

◆ **Figure 6.1** Factors involved in pitching and training workloads.

The challenge of this chapter is to reevaluate how pitchers prepare themselves for pitching a baseball. Quite simply, resistance training works. It is in everyone's best interest to implement a program that will help a pitcher peak for competition. Peaking is an interesting concept that is starting to get more attention in baseball. In the following section, Dr. John Gleddie addresses the subject.

ACHIEVING PEAK PITCHING PERFORMANCE

By John Gleddie, DC

Peaking is the process whereby an athlete's physiological, psychological, and biomechanical attributes reach a performance crescendo at the same time. Often, superior competitive performances result.

Producing a peak when needed is a constant challenge for you and your athlete. Until recently, weird theories and superstitious pregame behaviors were about all we had to explain the peaking process. Now we have a more objective tool: soft-tissue imaging. This tool gives us the ability to objectively measure an athlete's stress level in training and in competition. This information enables you to better predict your player's performance readiness.

Ideally, baseball pitchers would return to action only when their arms had fully recovered from the stresses of the previous competition. In reality, pitchers conform to a conventional five-day cycle that supposedly ensures enough rest and recovery time. The activities engaged in by the pitcher within this five-day cycle strongly influence the regeneration process.

Microcyles: Stress, Recovery, and Peaking

Recent thermographic studies have found that training stress in a pitcher's arm maximizes about 24 hours after the conclusion of the game. Recovery follows a steady and progressive course over the next four days.

There are exceptions to these two findings. One example is Nolan Ryan. Nolan's approach to recovery evolved through trial and error and has been reinforced by years of success.

Nolan interrupts the traditional recovery process by conducting a heavy weight-training program during the initial 24-hour postgame period. This imposes a greater systemic fatigue on his system, lengthens the recovery period somewhat, and would appear to achieve a higher overcompensation state. When this cycle works well, Nolan produces outstanding pitching performances. It isn't recommended for most pitchers, however, especially pitchers with poor mechanics or pitchers who can get excessively sore after they've competed. Give the body time to heal wounds before the heavier lift.

A CASE STUDY OF PITCHER PEAKING: MICROCYCLE MANAGEMENT

Kevin Brown is an example of pitcher peaking. By altering his weight-training days and his skill-work days, we managed to lessen his stress-grade level and peak him more efficiently. A two-year, thermographic window of Brown's microcycle appears in figure 6.2. It shows how and why we varied his resistance training and skill work to optimize his peaking for a start. This profile optimizes the interaction of competition and preparation by fine-tuning pitching mechanics, throwing workloads, and physical conditioning to fit his physiological makeup.

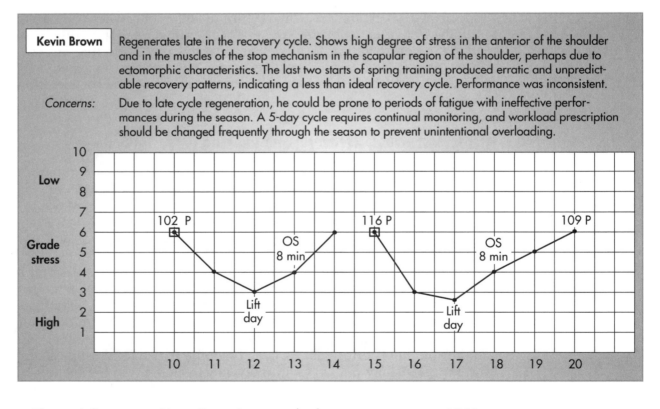

Kevin Brown Regenerates late in the recovery cycle. Shows high degree of stress in the anterior of the shoulder and in the muscles of the stop mechanism in the scapular region of the shoulder, perhaps due to ectomorphic characteristics. The last two starts of spring training produced erratic and unpredictable recovery patterns, indicating a less than ideal recovery cycle. Performance was inconsistent.

Concerns: Due to late cycle regeneration, he could be prone to periods of fatigue with ineffective performances during the season. A 5-day cycle requires continual monitoring, and workload prescription should be changed frequently through the season to prevent unintentional overloading.

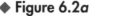 **Figure 6.2a**   Kevin Brown's microcyle during spring training 1991.   *(continued)*

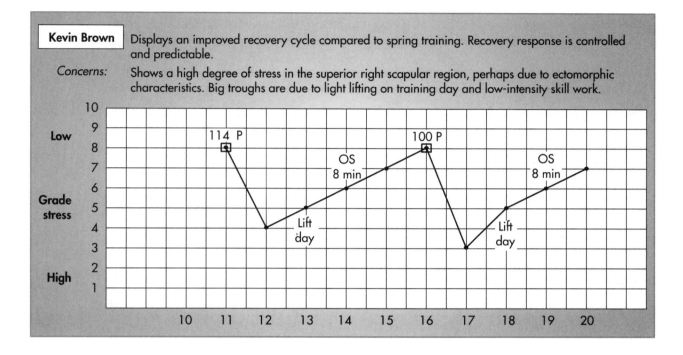

◆ **Figure 6.2b** *(continued)* Kevin Brown's microcycle during July 1991.

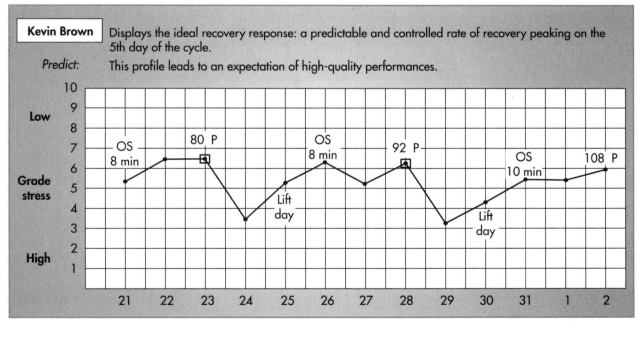

◆ **Figure 6.2c**   Kevin Brown's microcycle during spring training 1992.   *(continued)*

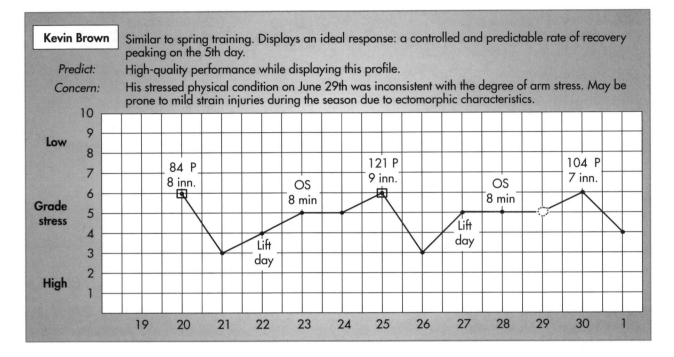

◆ **Figure 6.2d** *(continued)* Kevin Brown's microcycle during June 1992.

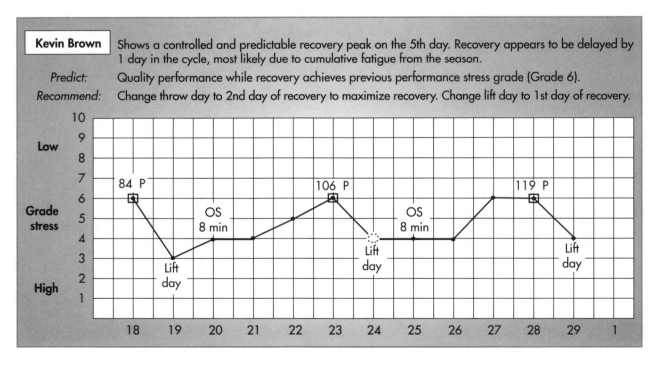

◆ **Figure 6.2e**   Kevin Brown's microcycle during August 1992.

This section by Dr. Gleddie typifies microcycle management for a starting pitcher. Now you have some insight into what a successful major-league starter goes through 30 to 35 times per year. Successful major-league relievers will vary the same basic process with less intensity but more frequency. A relief pitcher's microcycle appears in figure 6.3.

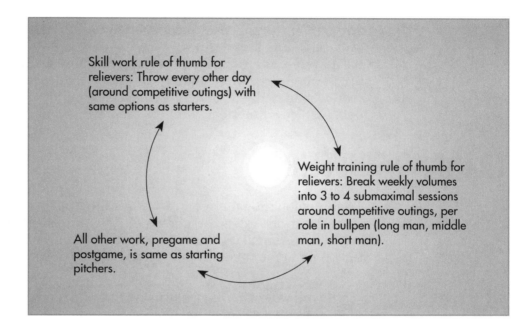

Skill work rule of thumb for relievers: Throw every other day (around competitive outings) with same options as starters.

Weight training rule of thumb for relievers: Break weekly volumes into 3 to 4 submaximal sessions around competitive outings, per role in bullpen (long man, middle man, short man).

All other work, pregame and postgame, is same as starting pitchers.

 Figure 6.3   A relief pitcher's microcycle.

FUNCTIONAL TRAINING FOR PITCHERS

I learned the hard way that you cannot rubber-stamp a training program and instructional approach with every pitcher. Preparation is like a huge cookbook, and you are trying to find a recipe to fit your pitcher. The training meal has to be served to taste to be successful. (And remember, even Betty Crocker burns a brownie now and then!)

I've also learned the hard way that players must be held accountable for their training protocols. Here are the boundaries for functional cross-conditioning of pitchers.

STRENGTHEN THE WEAK LINKS

If pitchers are only as strong as their weakest link, then with equivalent mechanics and pitch totals the pitchers in the Pacific Rim *had* to be more functional in their muscle strength and endurance relationship. Their connective tissue and small-muscle groups had parity with their prime movers or large-muscle groups. In reality, they had connective tissue and small-muscle endurance with below average big-muscle or prime mover strength. They were also quite flexible. In absorbing, directing, and delivering energy from feet to middle fingertip out into baseball, their sequential muscle loading was efficient. Every link in the kinetic energy chain contributed equally. American pitchers, however, have prime-mover strength at the expense of connective tissues and small-muscle groups. Their absolute strength was dysfunctional and, therefore, their sequential muscle loading was inefficient. Certain links in the kinetic energy chain fired either disproportionately, or out of sequence, when absorbing, directing, and delivering energy from feet to middle fingertip out into baseball. Also, few American pitchers are flexible.

TRAINING GUIDELINES

Train for functional strength. Always integrate, never isolate and work three positions (straight, supinate, pronate) and three movements (linear, circular, angular). Work the total body *daily* with a single set and multiple reps in the different positions and movements. Choose these workouts:

- **Stamina work**, which consists of cardiorespiratory conditioning with cross-specific positions and movements with aerobic/anaerobic intensity.
- **Flexibility work** for joint integrity. Work joints and extremities in angles of 90 degrees to 180 degrees, and never hyperflex or hyperextend a joint in relation to torso (head and center of gravity). Do not stretch; it loosens joints, and throwing itself is a joint-loosening process—double jeopardy!
- **Bodywork**, or closed-chain work, for better balance between small, medium, and large muscle groups.
- **Connective tissue and muscle endurance work** for upper body with elastic cord and light dumbbells and for total body with elastic-cord training.

STAMINA WORK

Stamina work is both aerobic and an aerobic. We'll use plyos (plyometric exercises) and intervals in our program. *Intervals* are anaerobic exercises that can be easily performed on a ball field. A ball field breaks distance down perfectly as follows: foul line to centerfield = 110, foul pole to foul pole = 220, circle the park = 440. Our simple interval program breaks down as follows:

- Sprint a 110, walk a 110

- Sprint a 220, walk a 110
- Sprint a 330, walk a 110
- Sprint a 440, walk a 110
- Sprint a 330, walk a 110
- Sprint a 220, walk a 110
- Sprint a 110, walk a 110.

Briefly, plyos can be used as a warm-up *before* integrated flexibility to get core body temperature elevated. (The Germans call it an aerobic flush; their marathoners actually jog a mile or two before a marathon.) Plyos are aerobic at low intensity and long distance, anaerobic at high intensity, and quick steps over short distances (i.e., 90 feet). We perform four basic exercises:

- Forward run (jog)
- Backward run (jog)
- Flex-T kariokas
- High knee skips

The backward run helps the endurance of abs and low back for posture. The flex-T kariokas help the endurance of shoulders and arms.

FLEXIBILITY WORK

We'll work the legs, torso, and arms in this flexibility sequence. Remember to work the legs and arms in three different positions—straight, supinate, and pronate. In the supinate position, your feet will be pointed in, kind of like a pigeon. For the pronate position, your feet will be pointed out, kind of like a duck. As you stretch, it's important to work from *feet to fingertips* whenever possible. You'll use this sequence because the first sensory signal for pitching balance in movement comes from the balls and arches of your feet. Your brain processes this input and tries to align the head and belly button accordingly.

Narrow-Stance Leg Flex

As shown in figure 6.4, you assume the narrow position by balancing on the balls of your feet. Your knees are slightly flexed and your hands are on your knees to begin, and on your hips to finish. Your head remains slightly in front of and over your center of gravity. Flex your joints in the order listed below:

- Move linearly (that is, straight right and left) for three to five reps.
- Roll the joint in a circular motion (both right and left) for three to five reps.
- Roll the joint angularly, or in a figure-eight motion, for three to five reps.

Work from the ground up in the following progression:

1. Ankle joints.
2. Knee joints. (This is the only lower-body joint in this sequence to be worked at multiple angles, from a slight flex up to 90 degrees, but never more than 90 degrees.)
3. Hips.
4. Shoulders.
5. Elbows.

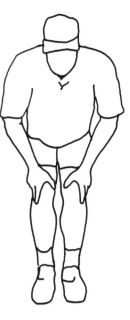

◆ **Figure 6.4**   The narrow stance ready position.

Medium Stance Leg Flex

Position A: As figure 6.5 shows, stand with your feet about 12 inches apart. Keep your balance on the balls of your feet with your knees flexed. Place your hands on knees and make sure your head remains slightly in front of and over your center of gravity. With your hands pushing on the sides of your knees

- move your knees linearly left and right for three to five reps,
- roll your knees in a circular motion in both directions for three to five reps, and
- roll your knees in a figure-eight motion for three to five reps.

◆ **Figure 6.5**   The medium stance ready position.

Position B: Assume the reverse toe-touch position as shown in figure 6.6. Your knees are bent and your hands are on the floor. You assume the finish position with your hands on the floor and your knees bent. Then you unbend your knees as much as you can (to tolerance) without lifting your hands from the floor. Follow this sequence:

- Perform three to five reverse toe touches with your toes pointing forward (straight position).
- Next, perform three to five reps with your toes pointing in (supinate position).
- Next, perform three to five reps with your toes pointing out (pronate position).

◆ **Figure 6.6**   The reverse toe touch in the medium stance with toes forward.

Position C: This is a squat in the flex-T position. Take the position shown in figure 6.7. Your hands are comfortably clasped in front of your shoulders in a flex-T to help with balance as you squat at the three positions. Keeping feet flat, squat down to tolerance with your head forward and over your belly button. Perform three to five repetitions in each of the three positions—straight, supinate (toes in), and pronate (toes out).

◆ **Figure 6.7**   Squats ready position with elbows in flex-T.

Wide-Stance Leg Flexes

Figure 6.8, *a–c* shows variations of the wide stance, which is what the Japanese call the *power pyramid.* Your knees are bent and your hands are flat on the floor.

- In the first position (figure 6.8*a*), perform three to five repetitions of "back push-ups" by straightening your knees and then bending them again. In the same position, move your bottom in a circle, both right and left, for three to five repetitions.
- Next, perform three to five hamstring stretches by leaning left and leaning right while keeping the toes straight (figure 6.8*b*).
- Next, modify the hamstring stretch by leaning right with your right foot pointed out, and then leaning left with your left foot pointed out (figure 6.8*c*).

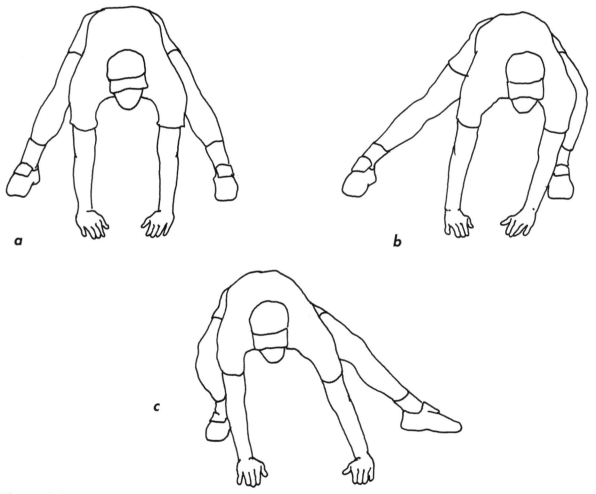

a

b

c

◆ **Figure 6.8,** *a–c*

Torso Flexes

For the various torso stretches, you will stand in a narrow stance with your hands on your hips. To stretch the torso, follow this progression:

- Perform hip circles (like doing a hula hoop) both left and right for three to five reps.
- Tilt your hips both right and left for three to five reps.
- Perform scapular shrugs by moving your shoulder blades up, forward, and backward (see figure 6.9).

◆ **Figure 6.9**

Arm Flexes

To stretch the arms, we'll perform a series of "saws." This movement mimics a sawing motion, with the elbows at 90 degrees. Both arms move at the same time in the same motion. Figure 6.11, *a–d* shows the different variations of the saw.

Position A: First perform saws forward and backward, with your arms at your sides and your palms open and thumbs up (figure 6.10*a*).

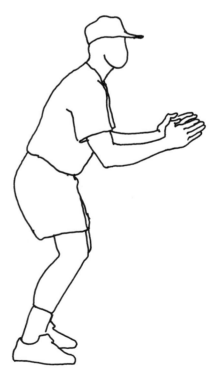

◆ **Figure 6.10***a*

Position B: Next, saw right over left in front of the stomach (see figure 6.10*b*). Perform this exercise with your palms open and thumbs up.

b

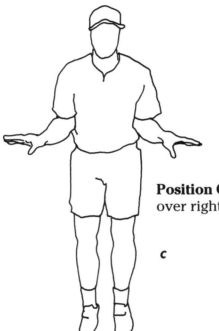

c

Position C: Keep elbows on rib cage, crossing right arm over left then left over right. Perform with palms up and palms down.

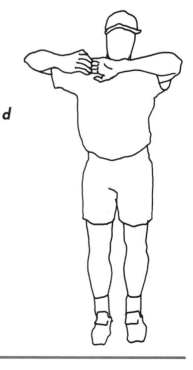

d

Position D: Finally, we'll modify this flex further by having you put your throwing hand in front of your eyes with your thumbs down. Clasp the fingers of your glove hand with the elbows in the flex-T and pull out to tolerance (see figure 6.10*d*). Circle and swim your shoulders forward and backward 3-5 reps. Repeat the flex, pushing in with hands, to tolerance.

◆ **Figure 6.10,** *b-d*

BODYWORK EXERCISES

These exercises are designed to for better balance between small, medium, and large muscle groups. These are closed-chain exercises, and exercises for both the upper and lower body are included.

Flex-T Push Ups

Perform flex-T push-ups with your hands straight, supinate (hands in), and pronate (hands out). You can do these in either the standard position or the modified position with your knees on the floor.

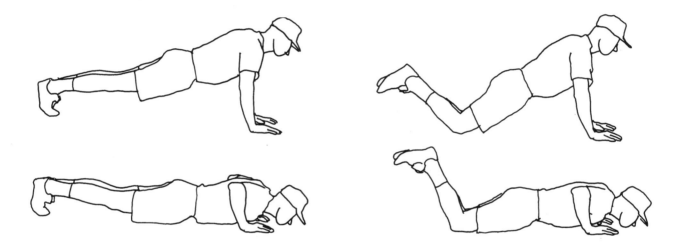

Butt-Ups

Perform butt-ups with your hands in the straight, supinate, and pronate positions. Extend your arms until the butt is off the ground, pinch your shoulder blades together, and return to the ground.

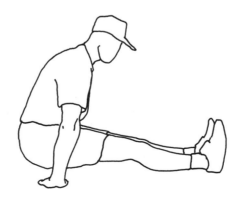

Side-Ups

Perform side-ups by turning your body on its side. Line up the ankles, knees, and hips, and stabilize the torso on a forearm in half of a flex-T. Place the other hand on the ground in front of the chest, lean into that hand until the backside "turns on," and then do one-arm push-ups to tolerance.

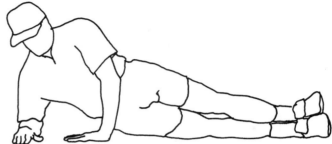

Elbow-Ups

Perform elbow-ups by lying on your back with hands resting on thighs. Use the elbows and triceps to lift the shoulders and head off the ground as high as possible. Hold for a count of five seconds, and then pinch the shoulder blades together five times. Return to the original position and move the hands to the belly button. Repeat the exercise with the following variations:

- Hands on the belly button
- Thumbs in the armpits
- Hands behind the head

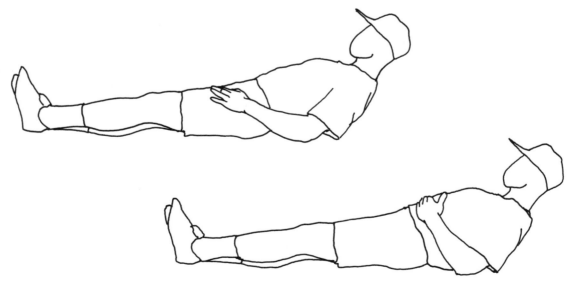

Cobras

Keep your belly button and legs flat on the ground and lift your torso up as high as you can. Think of yourself as a cobra about to strike. Press hard into the ground and hold for a count of five seconds, then pinch the shoulder blades together five times before returning to the original position. This exercise is performed with three variations:

- Hands in a flex-T position (see view *a*)
- Hands in a Y position (pronate) as in view *b*
- Hands in crossed in front of you under your chin (supinate) as in view *c*

a
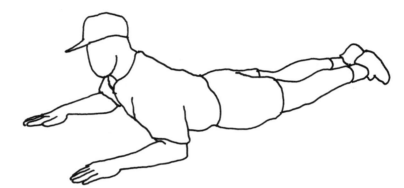

b
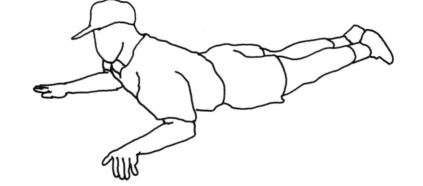

c
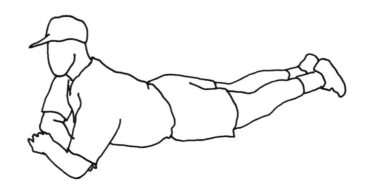

Forward Lunges

Perform forward lunges, bringing the knee to the belly button, then stride out to the ball of foot and land into a lunge. During the whole motion you should think "absorb, direct, and delivery the energy." After the forward lunges, perform a series of three to five backward lunges alternating the left and right feet going backward. Exaggerate the forward lean and tighten the abs before stepping back to maximize the benefit.

Side Lunges

Perform a series of three to five strides to the right, alternating with three to five strides to the left. On a side stride, cock your knee toward your belly button to absorb energy and stride to the right. At foot strike, you glide so that your torso and body weight continues linearly toward your direction of movement. When your torso and body weight has transferred to your right foot, you twist your trunk toward the direction of movement and squat. This trunk rotation should be delayed as long as possible (while still maintaining a fluid motion). The keys to remember are "stride, glide, and rotate late."

Step-Ups

Perform a series of step-ups onto a low step. Vary the height of the step to tolerance until it affects posture. Step up forward for three to five reps with the feet straight, pronate, and supinate. Repeat doing backward step ups facing away from the step.

Side Step-Downs

Step down off a low step to the side. Lift the knee to the belly button, step down, touch the ball of foot, and return to the original position without changing posture. Repeat to tolerance, then switch legs.

SIT-UP EXERCISES FOR TRUNK STABILIZATION

The following trunk stabilization and sit-up program is designed to work all muscle groups in the abdominal area. The lower back is always supported, and the trunk is stabilized. No disc or nerve problems should occur if properly exercised.

Bent-Leg Wall Sit-Ups

Lie on floor close enough to a wall so feet are flat against the wall and knees are bent at a 90-degree angle. Put hands behind head and lift upper body until elbows reach knees. Alternate right elbow to left knee, left elbow to right knee, keeping feet flush against the wall.

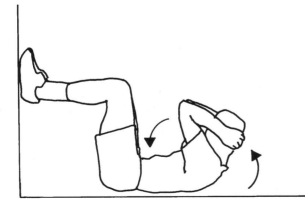
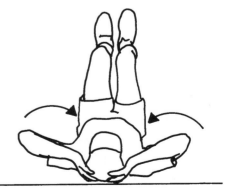

Straight-Leg Wall Sit-Ups

Lie on floor close enough to a wall so legs and buttocks are flush to surface of wall. Clasp hands together and reach to full extension over top of head. Lift upper body off ground, touch hands as high as possible on legs, keeping lower body flush to wall.

 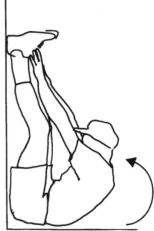

Wall Crunches

Lie on floor close enough to a wall so buttocks are touching wall. Arrange feet so soles are touching flush with each other in a yoga like position. Clasp hands on ears and crunch forward, trying to put nose on toes. Do until fatigue. Rest. Then crunch right elbow to left knee until fatigued. Rest. Then crunch left elbow to right knee until fatigued.

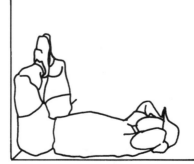 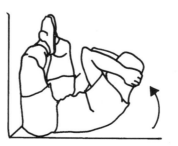 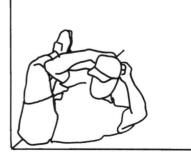

Feet Flat on Wall Crunches

Put feet flat against wall about six inches apart. Place buttocks as close to the wall as possible and keep knees about six inches apart. Put hands behind head, lift shoulders off the floor as high as possible, and hold them there. While in this position, push abdominal muscles and lower back through the floor, alternating with a "beat" of relaxation between pushes. Do repetitions to tolerance.

Floor Sit-Ups

Lie on floor with hands clasped behind head and legs bent at knees (at an angle that permits lower back and bottom of feet to be flat on floor). Lift upper body as high as possible off floor, keeping hands behind head. Lift lower body until knees touch elbows. Return upper body to floor followed by lower body until original position is reached.

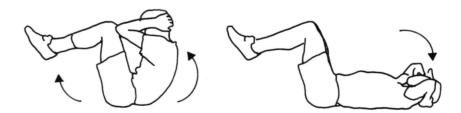

Floor Sit-Up Variations

Assume same starting position. Lift upper and lower body simultaneously to the point where elbows touch knees, then return to original position.

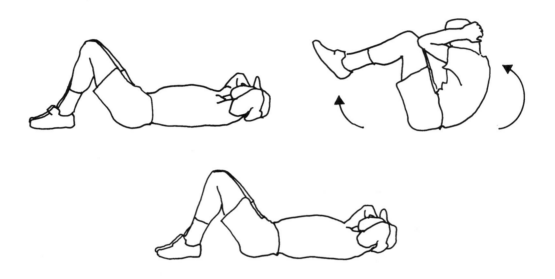

Assume same starting position. Lift upper body as high as possible, then lower body until elbows touch knees at that point. Extend legs and arms, trying to grab ankles with hands. Return upper body to floor followed by lower body until original position is reached.

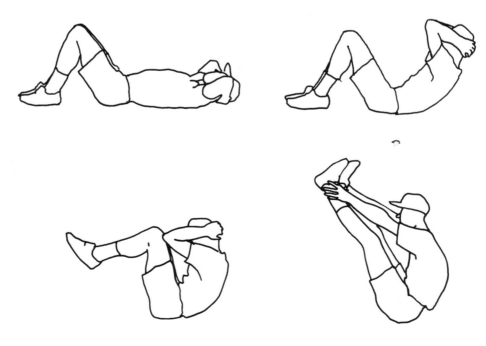

Assume same starting position. Lift lower body until legs and knees are at a 90° angle. Lift upper body until elbows touch knees. Bicycle legs with elbows touching opposite knees until fatigued and return to original position.

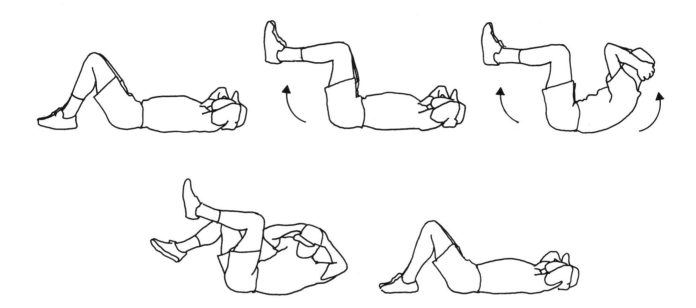

Lie fully stretched out on the floor with your feet together, toes to the sky, and hands together (palms up) as far as reach will allow above the head. Push abdominals and lower back flat against the floor and hold for a count of 30 seconds. Relax 10 seconds and repeat to fatigue.

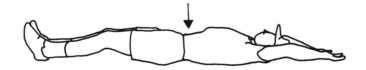

Lie fully stretched out on the floor, stomach down. In first set of 10, lift legs first, then arms into a superman position. In second set, lift arms first, then legs. In third set, lift both arms and legs at the same time. In fourth set, lift right arm and left leg. In fifth set, lift left arm and right leg. In sixth set, lift right arm and right leg, then left arm and left leg. In remaining sets, push abdominals into the floor and hold for 30 seconds. Relax 10 seconds and repeat to fatigue.

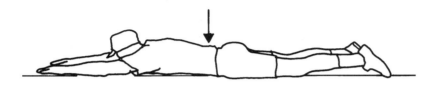

CONNECTIVE TISSUE AND MUSCLE ENDURANCE WORK

In 30-plus years of professional baseball, I have never hurt a prime mover (a large muscle or muscle group) while throwing a baseball, nor have I seen any other pitcher hurt a large-muscle group by just throwing. Pitchers' injuries invariably occur in connective tissue and small-muscle groups. To that end, whenever possible, prime movers should be trained after training connective tissue and small-muscle groups. Muscle balance and muscle endurance should be addressed before muscle strength, and functional strength should have priority over absolute strength.

This is a departure from the norm. Traditionally, resistance training has been prime-mover oriented with a focus on absolute strength. It hasn't worked for baseball. What does work is a program that incorporates connective tissue and muscle endurance work. We do this with light dumbbells and elastic-cord exercises.

Light Dumbbells

Light dumbbells—I call them training wheels—are 3- to 10-pound weights lifted in 12 sets at three angles of three to five reps or three rotations of three to five reps with intensity. Intensity means backing up sets, one right after another, allowing little or no rest between the movement sets. Within each dumbbell exercise, linear and rotational movements simulate fastball, breaking ball, and change-up forearm positions through a cross-specific range of motion with shoulders and elbows in each set.

The light dumbbells recruit blood flow to connective tissue and small muscle groups before big-muscle prime movers take over—sort of a reverse pyramiding effect. The sequencing and positioning of torso and limbs should always be cross-specific to the mechanics of pitching.

Exercise 1

Start with weights at tip of shoulders. Alternate extending arms to full reach. Option: Alternate rotating palms out or in during extension.

Exercise 2

Start with weights at sides. Bring right arm to left shoulder bending elbow, palm up going up, palm down coming down.

Exercise 3

Start with weights hanging behind head and shoulders with elbows held as high as possible. Alternate extending to full reach. Option: Do both arms at the same time but keep elbows as close to head as possible. When arms are extended, they should be slightly in front of or behind your head, not directly above.

Exercise 4

Start with weights hanging at sides. Lift across body at 45-degree angle to shoulder height. Alternate, keeping back of hand toward sky. Pretend shoulders are against a wall and keep them there with each lift. Option: Rotate thumbs down, thumbs up in the lift.

Exercise 5

Start with weights hanging at sides and lift straight out and up to full extension of arms overhead. Stretch shoulders and lower back when weights are fully extended. Option: Rotate thumbs forward with the lift and when returning hands to start position.

Exercise 6

Start with weights hanging at sides and lift away from body into a T position with arms fully extended. Have weights slightly forward of the shoulders and point thumbs down with the lift.

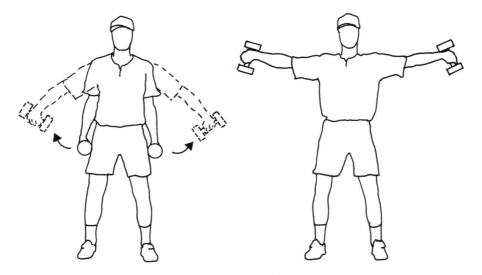

Exercise 7

Start with weights touching together in front of groin. Lift away from body in a windmill action, touching weights at a point in front of head (not over the top) with arms fully extended, and return slowly. Rotate palms down and out, then up and in as weights touch on top. Do the same going down. Remember to keep your arms slightly in front of your head.

Exercise 8

Bend over and let weights rest on floor in a toe-touch position. Alternate lifting weight to shoulder leaving opposite weight on floor. Option: Rotate thumbs forward or backward with each lift to tolerance.

Exercise 9

Bend over to an L position with belly button between knees. Bring elbows to shoulder height first, then extend arms straight out until parallel with ground. Keep arms extended and return to original position. Option: Rotate thumbs down with extension, then up with extension.

Exercise 10

Start with weights hanging at sides, palms facing back. Lift arms (together or one at a time) until elbow and forearm are at a 90-degree angle, then extend weight out and up to shoulder height. Reverse sequence to starting position. Option: Turn thumbs up in a hitchhike movement with the lift.

Exercise 11

Start with weights in a hands-up position. Keeping elbows parallel to ground, roll weights forward to shoulder height, pause, and roll weights back to shoulder height (or as far as possible.)

Exercise 12

Start with throwing-arm dumbbell in an elbow-shoulder-high, hitchhike-up position, and the opposite arm dumbbell in an across-the-body, thumb-down, and at-hip position. Take throwing arm to hip and opposite arm to hitchhike, making an X pattern with arms across the torso. Rotate thumb up to thumb down during movement.

Elastic-Cord Work

The elastic cord is a complement to the dumbbells because it can be isometric, as well as isotonic, work. Also, depending on how far the cord is stretched, resistance can be increased or decreased as a function of how the athlete feels in his workout (i.e., tolerance).

The elastic cord is a cross-specific mechanics-training and resistance-training device for both prehabilitation and rehabilitation. It can be used on and off the field, in any phase of preparation, for skill work or competition (i.e., as low-resistance, low-intensity activities for loosening up, as medium-resistance, medium-intensity activities for warming up, or as high-resistance, high-intensity activities for strength training). The key to the integrated protocol is in the sequencing and positioning of torso and limbs specific to the movements of the pitching mechanics you are training on the field (i.e., position specific, resistance specific, movement specific to tolerance, for whatever phase of preparation or recovery the player is in).

Elastic-cord work yields maximum return with minimum risk, and you are training skill while training strength. Elastic resistance training is an important part of a pitcher's workout continuum, both in-season and off-season. Anchor your cord to a post or weight machine to perform the following exercises.

Table 6.1 shows pounds of torque for each color of Xertube elastic cord that you will use. Torque give a good indication of the actual work done when training with elastic resistance.

Table 6.1	**Pounds of Torque Using Elastic Resistance**

Green

2 x original length (24 in.) = 11.5 ft-lb of torque
3 x original length (36 in.) = 18.0 ft-lb of torque
4 x original length (48 in.) = 23.0 ft-lb of torque
5 x original length (60 in.) = 52.0 ft-lb of torque

Red

2 x original length (24 in.) = 11.5 ft-lb of torque
3 x original length (36 in.) = 14.0 ft-lb of torque
4 x original length (48 in.) = 18.0 ft-lb of torque
5 x original length (60 in.) = 61.5 ft-lb of torque

Blue

2 x original length (24 in.) = 11.5 ft-lb of torque
3 x original length (36 in.) = 27.0 ft-lb of torque
4 x original length (48 in.) = 52.0 ft-lb of torque
5 x original length (60 in.) = 72.0 ft-lb of torque

Note: From a Cybex Tensile strength study (1988). The Sport Performance Rehabilitation Institute (SPRI) researched, developed, and marketed Xertube. A one-foot piece of tubing attached to a fence strap was used for this study.

High Elbow Swims

Perform a set of 5 to 15 reps facing forward, followed by a set facing away from the anchor. Option: Do a set with thumbs up, then a set with thumbs down.

Hitchhikes

Perform a set of 5 to 15 reps with the right arm, followed by a set with the left arm. Option: For one set, perform the movement going from thumbs down to thumbs up. For the next set, go from thumbs up to thumbs down.

Thumbs-Up, Thumbs-Down Pulls

Pull with both arms at the same time. Perform 5 to 15 reps with the thumbs up, then do 5 to 15 reps with the thumbs down.

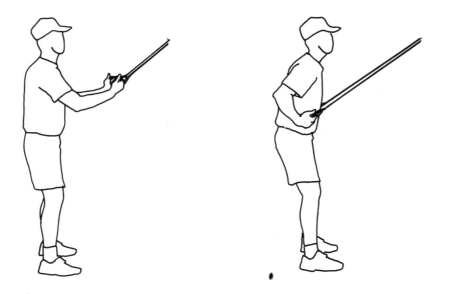

Why Me's

Face away from the anchor and pull the cords in front of your body. The thumbs should go from a down position to an up position.

As we wind down this chapter on training programs and tools for pitchers, remember the importance of *function*. Good, old Confucius had it right even before baseball was invented when he said, "The superior man is firm in the right way, and not merely firm." When training the arm for strength to pitch a baseball, it should be functional strength, skill-specific to pitching a baseball. And as mentioned in the introduction to this section, it should be a balanced strength that will meet the challenge of matching throwing workloads with whatever mechanical efficiency the athlete can master. We know that an athlete pays a significant price to pitch a baseball.

We know that training the arm is putting money in the bank or pitches back into the arm. Building and maintaining a reserve in a player's pitch bank should be a common goal for coach and pitcher. It must be emphasized, however, that resistance training for pitching is different from resistance training for other sports. In an era of enhancement chemicals like growth hormone, steroids, DHEA, and creatine, please understand that.

WEIGHT TRAINING FOR PITCHERS IS NOT BODYBUILDING

Functional, balanced strength, not bulk, is the goal. Therefore, work small groups and connective tissues first. Give them the most attention in all the macrocycles. Why? Pitchers seldom, if ever, get hurt in a big-muscle group. It is always tendinitis, ligamentitis, strained teres major, pulled infraspinatus, or torn rotator cuff—never a pulled pectoralis or latissimus dorsi. See the logic?

So unlike traditional weight lifting, reverse the pyramid and work small to large. This has a residual benefit of building muscle density rather than muscle bulk. Because the "little guys" have been worked before the prime movers, they have received their share of oxygen and nutrients before the "big guys." This small to large progression also helps to alleviate the problem of muscle tissue building faster than connective tissue and bone. Hypertrophic parity, or balance of muscle, tendon, ligament, and bone, is achieved more readily.

Even on heavy lifting days, start with integrated flexibility, bodywork, light dumbbells, and elastic cord. Think of it as a warm-up. Call the little dumbbells "training wheels" on heavy days. You might be saying, "Well that's great, but we are not big leaguers. We don't have a million-dollar weight room to work out in, or the time to do it. We've got school classes, a limited budget, and limited access to a weight-training facility." To that I say, don't make excuses! You can outfit your pitchers with a mobile weight room very inexpensively. A few pairs of 5- to 10-pound dumbbells, a couple of elastic cords with grips attached, and your body will do it!

I often am asked which is better: dumbbells, elastic cord, or bodywork? Well, the stress on a muscle group when worked to tolerance can be virtually the same with dumbbells or elastic cord. In equation form:

Weight + repetition + range of motion =
tension on cord + repetition + amount of time each stretch is held + range of motion

Table 6.2 on page 98 compares dumbbells, elastic cord, and bodywork exercises for small muscle groups and connective tissue.

INJURY PREVENTION FOR PITCHERS

Richard Heitsch, MD, FASC

Several years ago it became increasingly apparent that my stepson had considerable talent as a pitcher. I became interested in using my medical background to help him avoid injuries that could prevent him from realizing his potential. Although I had no problem applying medical literature, I had very little knowledge of the fine points of baseball or of the injuries specific to pitching. There was a lot to learn. Learning what I could and applying it to a practical situation turned out to be one of my most re-

Table 6.2	**Bodywork Comparison Chart**		
	Type of exercise	**Workload**	**Exercise efficiency**
Dumbells	Isotonic: Variable resistance through range of motion with each of 12 exercises involving arm and upper body.	A function of the dumbbell weight, number of repetitions, and the speed of movement through range of motion. Energy is expended by various muscle groups involved.	Good to excellent with proper supervision. With improper supervision, there is risk of injury caused by too much weight per exercise or improper technique. The movements involved with these exercises are related more closely to the muscle memories of throwing.
Elastic cord	Isotonic or isometric: Variable resistance with movement or fixed-arm and upper-body positioning. It is isometric if there is no movement involved in any of the exercises.	A function of tension, the tensile strength of the elastic cord, and how long each stretch is held. The tensile strength of the cord we use starts resisting at approximately 3 pounds and maxes out at about 45 pounds. Energy is expended to hold each stretch position. Muscle, tendon, and ligament strength is maintained or increased by working to a level of tolerance with each stretch.	Good to excellent if all muscle groups involved in the throwing motion are worked in a daily routine. There is little risk of injury because resistance is uniform per cord elasticity and stretch length.
Bodywork using your body	Isotonic or isometric: Closed-chain resistance and function of movement or fixed position.	When doing bodywork on the horizontal plane, feet *below* belly button, resistance = 60 percent of body weight. Feet *even* with belly button, resistance = 80 percent of bodyweight. Feet *above* belly button, resistance = 100 percent of body weight. Reps to tolerance.	Excellent. You can do position-specific, movement-specific bodywork year-round because muscle failure is not a factor and the risk of injury is minimal.

warding experiences. This is written in the hope that some of what I have learned might help other young athletes, especially pitchers, to avoid certain injuries.

The best starting point seemed to be an understanding of what happens during the physical act of throwing a pitch. Although this is a very complex activity involving multiple body parts and muscle groups and occurring at very high speed, researchers using high-speed photography have been able to capture it and break it down to basic segment, as Tom House has done in part I of this book.

By slowing down the process of pitching with this high-speed video photography, we find that

- deceleration is accomplished in half the time of acceleration
- the pitching hand finishes palm out, regardless of the pitch thrown

• forward movement off the pitching rubber is most effective when it is a controlled fall rather than a pushing off with the leg.

Although breaking down the pitching motion into many component parts is helpful in understanding what happens, pitchers don't throw in several discrete phases; they throw in one continuous sequence of motion. This continuous movement results from the forces generated when muscles contract to create movement around joints. It is called sequential muscle loading, defined when the cumulative forces of any contracting muscle group involved in the throw are added to the forces generated in preceding body parts and passed on to the next part. In other words, forward forces are generated in succession by the forward fall off the mound, turning the torso to face forward, and straightening the arm at the elbow. At this point the sum total of forward forces generated is applied to the ball and the pitch is released.

The process doesn't stop here, however, because deceleration begins at the release point. All forward forces must be slowed and eventually stopped. This phase is accomplished when the opposite muscle groups of acceleration take over and sequentially reverse the forward force.

Pitching injuries result when the pitching motion exceeds the ability of a given structure to withstand the applied forces. This can happen suddenly with a single application of force (acute injury), or it may be over a long period with repeated application of lesser force (overuse injury).

The most important factors in avoiding injury in pitchers are mechanics and balanced strength. As Tom has pointed out, technique, or mechanics, includes not only the proper performance of the individual movements involved in pitching but also the proper timing of each movement in the sequence. Good mechanics is necessary for the smooth and orderly transfer of force from the plant foot through the body and up the arm to the hand where the accumulated force is transmitted to the ball at the release point. Good mechanics results in force being directed straight toward home plate, avoiding any lateral movement that can detract from forward forces and decrease ball velocity. Good mechanics distributes stress over component body parts so that it is not concentrated at any one point, thereby reducing the likelihood of injury to that part.

The Body

Other factors will impede the proper performance of the individual movements involved in pitching. Fatigue, weakness, or a preexisting injury to any body part may cause alteration of mechanics and result in injury to another body part in the chain.

It is intuitively obvious that if one of a pair of oppositely acting muscles is much stronger than the other, the weaker of the pair is at increased risk to be overpowered and injured. Therefore, pitchers need balanced strength in each pair of muscles to avoid injury. When this balance of strength is not maintained, involved muscles can be injured and various secondary injuries can occur because of loss of stability at the involved joint. To understand where pitching-related injuries can occur, one has only to consider the relative size of body part, the amount of force applied, and the opportunity for mechanical error.

Legs

The larger muscles of the legs are subjected only to the force they themselves generate. They are the first link involved in the kinetic chain of a pitcher's delivery.

Trunk

Trunk muscles are sometimes damaged when excessive force strains them or pulls them away from their bony attachments. Trunk stabilization exercises will usually minimize risk of injury to any or all muscles in the torso. The torso, in effect, is passing force on to the arms, and it is not a mechanical problem when injury occurs.

Shoulder

The muscles of the shoulder are relatively small, are subjected to large accumulated force generated by several preceding muscle groups, and are very susceptible to injuries because of mistakes in mechanics. The shoulder's complex structure and the activity it is asked to perform in pitching compounds the likelihood of injury.

The shoulder is the weak link in a pitcher's body. To make matters worse, the shoulder responds poorly to treatment, and shoulder injuries are often career ending. For all these reasons, the most prudent approach in dealing with the shoulder is prevention. Learn good mechanics and build proper strength before increasing throwing workloads.

For me, when all is said and done, the focus of attention for injury prevention in pitching should be on the shoulder. It means finding better ways to identify and correct mechanical flaws, and better ways to develop and maintain strength in the muscles that accelerate and decelerate the shoulder.

Elbow

The large muscles of the upper arm control movement of the elbow. In pitching, this joint serves only to extend the arm. Elbow injuries usually involve tendons and are usually the result of mistakes in mechanics. Surgery for elbow tendon injuries has been quite successful in returning pitchers to their former level of performance.

Strength Training

Many baseball people have long been opposed to weight lifting and related methods of strength training. They contend that such methods result in decreased flexibility and cause injuries. Their concerns are appropriate, but such problems are avoidable.

To achieve the desired effect, the training program for a serious pitcher should start at around age 15, should include general body fitness, aerobic fitness, and strength training, should be designed to increase strength while maintaining flexibility, and should emphasize strengthening identified weak points such as the back of the shoulder. All major opposing muscle groups used in pitching should be exercised in order to develop and maintain balanced strength along the entire chain of transmitted force used in pitching.

The bad things that happen with strength training are generally related to two mistakes: not taking it seriously enough to learn proper technique and yielding to the temptation to see how much weight one can lift. Good technique includes mechanics and proper concentration. Every repetition of every exercise should be performed with concentration on complete range of motion and proper mechanicial technique with a weight that remains under control through the last repetition, and with the knowledge of what the exercise is designed to accomplish. There should be a minimum of wasted time with rapid progression from one exercise to the next through a carefully predesigned program.

Concentration should be nearly as intense as in game situations during a 60- to 90-minute workout three or four times a week. In this way a good foundation of mental and physical preparedness is laid while working toward injury prevention during both strength training and game situations.

Strength training will certainly not prevent all injuries, but it will decrease the likelihood of many. At present the Achilles heel of pitchers continues to be weakness in the back side of the shouder, particularly the rotator cuff. By the time pitchers are 17 or 18, rotator-cuff injuries are appearing with increasing frequency in those who have continued to pitch in organized baseball. How to prevent this is not clear. (Even New York Mets pitching coach Mel Stottlemyre, who told me his major-league career was ended by a rotator cuff injury, was unable to prevent the same career-ending injury in one of his two talented sons.)

Injury prevention must begin early by limiting the number of pitches thrown by those in their early years of organized baseball. For individuals who continue to pitch in organized ball, pitch limits should continue, and active conditioning programs, especially strength training, should be instituted at age 14 or 15.

CHAPTER 7

Transfer of Training to Performance

"Quite simply, today's pitchers don't throw enough.
Notice I said *throw*, not pitch."

Throughout the book, I've stressed the importance of throwing workloads, because combining flat-ground and mound work is part of the preparation equation. Competing injury-free and throwing strikes with three pitches should be both the goal and the ultimate reward for a properly prepared pitcher. But, as always, there are questions and concerns. For example: Can a pitcher throw too much? Can he play other positions, when not pitching, without risking arm problems? And, finally (the one most often asked by parents, coaches, and players), are there guidelines for pitch totals?

This short chapter addresses these questions and more. It provides current information about the physiology of throwing, the final piece of training for performance in competition.

PRACTICE THROWING

Baseball is a skill sport. Throwing on flat-ground and pitching on a mound require skill. Prepare correctly. The more an athlete throws and pitches properly, the better his skills will be. Flat-ground throwing takes less out of an arm than mound throwing. Remember from the introduction that when a pitcher's body absorbs, directs, and delivers energy, there's two-thirds less stress on the arm working on flat ground than on a hill. Quite simply, today's pitchers don't throw enough. Notice I said *throw*, not pitch. You don't see kids throwing or playing catch anymore unless it's in a structured practice or game situation. It's not really their fault. They get in trouble for throwing rocks, and just playing catch with a buddy (or a dad) is boring compared to a Nintendo play station or an electronic whatever. So is throwing a tennis ball against a garage door, or a whiffle ball in the backyard. The bottom line is that although athletes are bigger, faster, and stronger than ever, they just don't *play* enough or *throw* enough to develop baseball skills. We are asking them to pitch in competition before they've even learned how to throw. Coaches must get the most skill work possible out of a structured practice, and players must be encouraged to practice throwing on their own.

Pitching off a mound is a tearing-down process. A major leaguer, or a Little Leaguer, can lose up to 20 percent of his absolute arm strength because downhill deceleration is a shoulder- and elbow-joint loosener. And even with skill, strength, endurance, and stamina a major leaguer's or Little Leaguer's arm will start experiencing muscle failure at about 75 pitches. (Stresses are relative to the genetics of body weight and arm speed.) Properly prepared, a pitcher can accommodate this muscle failure with minimal cumulative wear and tear, pitching another 30 to 45 pitches per game *if* the pitcher gets to those totals at 15 to 20 pitches per inning. A large number of pitches in one inning (35-40) will cause as much wear and tear on an arm as a whole game at 15 to 20 pitches. And finally, it takes about 48 to 72 hours for an arm to recover from the muscle failure of mound work.

With this information in mind, we can now answer our earlier questions. Properly prepared, a pitcher can *pitch* too much off a mound. He cannot, however, *throw* too much on flat-ground. He can play other positions before and after pitching off a mound, with minimal risk of injury, because it's flat-ground throwing. Two final points: pay attention to the pitch-total parameters outlined and adjust according to each pitcher's mechanics, muscle strength and endurance, and stamina; and don't allow competitive mound work inside 72 hours if a pitcher is recovering from muscle failure.

To compete on the mound, Kevin Brown first mastered pitching mechanics on flat ground.

HOUSE RULES

Master pitching mechanics on flat-ground and compete on the mound. The same biomechanical movements are required of each, and you can pitch more with less physiological stress if you practice windup and stretch on the flat.

- Throw, throw, and throw with short, medium, and long toss to tolerance. Distance magnifies mechanical mistakes and increases risk of injury due to poor strength, low endurance, or muscle failure. Tolerance means athletes should throw at distances where perfect mechanics and functional strength and endurance match up. (A small, weak athlete with poor mechanics should throw at shorter distances; an athlete in muscle failure from a previous outing should throw only at that distance where stiffness or soreness doesn't affect mechanics.)

- Practice frequency and duration of pitching as a function of job description. Relievers should prepare working fewer pitches more often; starters should prepare with more pitches less often.

- Muscle failure for both starters and relievers should be repaired with ice, aerobics, and resistance training. Ice critical joints and muscles to stop the bleeding in tissues caused by microtears from the trauma of pitching. Use aerobic activity to flush lactic acid from muscle tissue—the residue left after an interaction between oxygen and the chemicals of a neuromuscular contraction. Use resistance training to bring oxygen and nutrients to muscles and connective tissue (in season) or maintenance. Do not push to muscle failure with resistance training until the off-season when skill in competition isn't a factor.

TRAINING WRAP-UP

At this point we've matched up technique and training with our information and instruction exchange. You've been shown what conditioning coaches, trainers, and physical therapists are doing to functionally cross-train strength, endurance, and stamina specific to pitching a baseball. You've also learned the physiological effects of throwing versus pitching workloads on flat-ground and mound. In combination, you now have a number of protocols to functionally integrate techniques of mechanical conditioning with the training of physical conditioning. Again, with a little of your coaching inspiration or your athletic motivation, you have new cutting-edge rules and tools to better prepare for pitching health and success in competition.

PART III

MENTAL AND EMOTIONAL ESSENTIALS

"I always enjoy asking coaches and athletes, 'Which comes first: success or confidence?' The audience is usually split 50-50. But neither side is correct or incorrect, because *preparation* comes first."

Baseball is a game of failure, coached by negative people in a misinformation environment. Mental and emotional makeup is the players' support system for physical competence in competition: a measure of his *persistence* as much as his *performance*. Historically, in baseball, the best hitters in the game fail 7 out of 10 times. The best pitchers fail or break even (with no decisions) 5 out of 10 times. It's obvious that in a game of failure, if the best pitchers fail less than the best hitters, then the game statistically favors pitching. A pitcher's mental toughness and emotional management must be based on the premise that by the law of large numbers *good pitching beats good hitting*. And while it's nice to throw a fastball in the mid-90 mph range, it isn't necessary. Good pitching is three pitches, something hard, something soft, and something that breaks, to two locations, in or away with late movement. Let's assume mechanics are sound and conditioning is functional. Then for coach and athlete the chapters in part III are all dedicated to the preparation and maintenance of mentally and emotionally managing our "good pitching beats good hitting" premise in competition. It can be taught, it can be learned, and a coach or pitcher doesn't need a PhD in psychology to master the process. I tell pitchers their brain is the software, or floppy disk, and their body is the hardware, or mainframe. Unless their floppy disk directs their mainframe properly, it's garbage in, garbage out. Bad thinking in a mechanically sound, functionally strong pitcher means more competitive failure than is statistically necessary. Know that proper preparation prevents poor performance. The mental software that drives that physical hardware of a competitive athlete must be properly programmed. By properly programming, I mean optimal focus and motivation.

Many sport psychologists emphasize positive visualization. This imaging technique can be very effective in the preparation phase if the athlete is imaging realistically. Visualizing yet-to-be performed or unrealistic feats can be bad for an athlete; it creates a double bind. Unless he has properly prepared his natural talent mechanically, physically, and nutritionally, no amount of visualization will allow him to actualize performance. Even if prepared he must have the opportunity for experience. Players can be taught information and given instruction, but they must gain their own experience and have at least enough natural talent to compete.

I tell coaches and players that playing in the major leagues is a wonderful vision and dream, but performing up to potential is a prerequisite in the world of competitive sports. So to realize the dream, an athlete must first deal with reality. The reality? It's integrating the components of preparation that will optimize a pitcher's interaction of confidence in competition with success in competition. (See figure III.1.)

Circle of Success

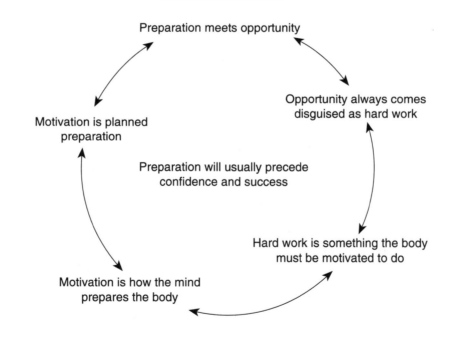

◆ **Figure III.1**   The circle of success model illustrates the relationship between a pitcher's preparation, confidence, and success.

The circle reveals how the physical processes involved in preparation match up with the mental processes involved in preparation. Visualization, then, becomes more specific to the competitive task at hand. For pitchers, it boils down to one pitch at a time: a total mental and physical commitment to this pitch in this situation. Opportunity creates experience, and visual imaging can be actualized consistently in competition only when the body is prepared to perform in a positive manner toward a positive thought.

The best pitcher doesn't always win; the pitcher who pitches best does. Proper thinking is the final piece of our performance trinity. Combined with proper technique and proper training, any pitcher can increase the probability of pitching his best in competition.

CHAPTER 8

Strategic Command

"Fifty percent of this game is 90 percent mental."
Yogi Berra

This chapter requires an intellectual commitment. There's really no emotion involved. Statistically, this is a series of "ifs and thens" that have been proven valid over the last 125-plus years of competitive baseball. Strategies are designed to increase a pitcher's probability of success in competition. Tactics are the physical implementation of a pitcher's strategic design. If he can command his tactics then he has strategic command on the mound. We've all heard the phrase "he's got command" used to describe a winning pitcher. In this chapter I'll tell coach and player how to design and implement strategies and tactics. Every successful pitcher I've observed, either foreign or domestic, amateur or professional, at any level of competition, consciously or unconsciously, has a strategic plan and the tactics to work his plan. If you don't have a plan try this: Throw strike one to every hitter, get the lead-off hitter in every inning, and put up a 0 in the inning after your team scores a run. This worked quite well for 28 years with a guy named Nolan Ryan!

STRATEGIES FOR OUTS

Throw strikes! Successful pitching is predicated on strikes. Even the wrong pitch thrown for a strike is better than the right pitch thrown for a ball.

Know your pitching strengths for *today*. Based on your warm-up, what is your "command pitch?" What is your "out" pitch? What is your "show me" pitch? What is your "get back in the count" pitch?

Know that you must throw all your pitches in competition to master those pitches in competition. Throwing them in practice does not guarantee mastery during a game.

Know your hitters' fastball weakness. Is the hitter a high-ball hitter or a low-ball hitter? Can he hit a ball inside or outside? The slower your fastball the more you must pitch in or in-off to own the plate. Half the plate is his, half the plate is yours—don't let him take your half away from you. Also, the slower your fastball, the greater the speed difference must be with your change-up.

Know that there are good breaking-ball hitters, but nobody hits a good breaking ball. Throw your breaking ball!

Know that no hitter has been taught to hit off-speed; every swing is geared toward hitting the fastball. Throw your off-speed pitch.

Throw your pitches in these percentages: 65 percent fastball, 20 percent breaking ball, 15 percent off-speed. Adjust to the moment. If you can't locate, change speeds. If you can't change speeds, locate. If you can't do either, at least be wild in the strike zone; it will put the ball in play.

Throw your pitches one at a time; there's stuff before the pitch and there's stuff after the pitch, but when it's time to make a pitch, give total physical and mental commitment to *this pitch this moment.*

Know the odds are in your favor. Three pitches to two locations means the hitter has to guess right out of 6 choices to hit the ball. Las Vegas

Randy Johnson knows that success is predicated upon throwing strikes. The wrong pitch thrown for a strike is better than the right pitch thrown for a ball.

would love those odds! The plate is *wide* early in the count and behind in the count. It *narrows* to the corners ahead in the count. Play the game mentally with your catcher *before* the game. Plan how to pitch each hitter on the opposing team and then let the game play itself by following your plan. If you don't have a scouting report on opposing teams hitters, you and your catcher should go watch the opposition take batting practice. (Two heads are better than one.) Decide where to locate your fastball with this in mind: hitters stand in the box to (1) see the ball better or (2) reach what they see better. In general, choose location according to how hitters position themselves at the plate.

1. "Stand-tall hitters" are *low*-ball hitters.
2. "Squat hitters" are *high*-ball hitters.
3. "Stand close to the plate hitters" like the ball *in*.
4. "Stand away from the plate hitters" like the ball *away*.

Pitch a short-armed hitter *in off* the plate when you want to go in. Don't throw him in for strikes. By the same token, pitch a long-armed hitter *away off* the plate when you want to go away. Throw all your pitches, but go to your command pitch to get ahead (unless you're pitching around the hitter). There are, however, optimal counts for certain pitch selections.

WORK THE COUNT

Optimal breaking ball counts are 0-0, 1-2, 0-2. An 0-0 breaking ball is a "get me over pitch. Statistically, 0-0 breaking balls put in play by a hitter result in a .078 batting average. A 1-2 or 0-2 breaking ball should look like a strike and break to the black or just off the plate.

Optimal off-speed counts are 1-0, 2-0, 2-1. If you have reasonable command of your off-speed pitch, any time a fastball is in order, a change-up is in order. You don't have to locate a change because off-speed is your weapon. Location and movement are a bonus if you get it.

Situation counts can work for you. For example, *base-stealing* counts are breaking ball, off-speed counts, with fast runners and no power at the plate in a close game. Vary your moves and your delivery time to the plate but throw *your* pitch.

Hit-and-run counts are fastball counts with average or below-average runners and a no-power, contact hitter at the plate in a close game. Vary your moves and your delivery time to the plate but throw your pitch. If you do have off-speed command, quick step and throw your change-up; you'll get a swinging strike and an out at second!

If you strategically plan your work and tactically work your plan, then you'll have command in competition. Statistically, over time, wins or losses will happen as a function of your skill and talent base against the hitters' skill and talent base. Remember, a prepared pitcher who mentally commits to the numbers and their probabilities will keep himself and his team in games.

"It's no fun throwing fastballs to guys who can't hit them. The real challenge is getting them out on stuff they can hit!"

Sam McDowell, Texas Ranger Employee Assistance Programs counselor and Cleveland Indians pitcher (1961-1971) in a pregame conversation at Arlington Stadium, 1992

I had to laugh. Sam McDowell is very entertaining with his story telling, and if you listen carefully, he is very insightful. For me, the important words from his statement above are fun, challenge, and getting them out. Getting them out is the purpose of pitching at any level.

Now that you have an intellectual foundation for pitching, let's move on to the mental and emotional belief system that supports it. Chapter 9 on concentration details some new psychological protocols.

HOUSE RULES

The following rules will help you gain confidence and become successful:

- **Set priorities.** You should know what is important and work on your priorities with a structured approach.
- **Take on problems.** Problems are opportunities in disguise and are roadblocks only if you allow them to be.
- **Set and demand standards of excellence.** You should know what you are striving for.
- **Work with a sense of urgency.** Nothing gets done with procrastination.
- **Pay attention to relevant details.** Ignore everything else.
- **Commit.** You should commit yourself and try not to compromise your commitments. Anyone can find an excuse for not following a commitment if he looks hard enough.
- **Don't worry.** You shouldn't waste time worrying about the things you can't control.
- **Understand, don't fear, failure.** Look at failures, examine them, but don't be resigned to them.
- **Work with emotions.** Learn to make your emotions work for you, not against you.
- **Have fun.** Fun is great therapy.

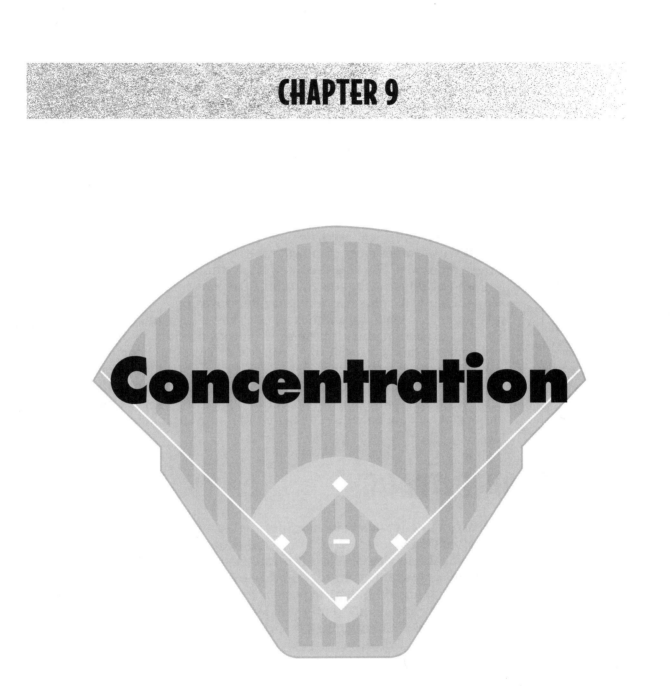

CHAPTER 9

Concentration

Problem: "Don't bother me, I'm concentrating."
Solution: "If you were concentrating, you couldn't be bothered."

The word *concentrate* is quite often misused and misinterpreted in sports. Coaches are always telling their athletes to concentrate, and most athletes are totally sincere in their attempts at concentration. But if they think they are concentrating, they're *not!* Concentration is a process, not a singular event. This process is actually a managed interaction between mind, body, and task. Done properly this managed interaction is a bonus in competition. Done improperly, as an event or a process, a serious double bind is created. For example, a typical coach/pitcher interaction will follow along these conversation lines: "Concentrate on the catcher's glove, John, visualize yourself throwing strikes." Sounds pretty good, doesn't it? Well, it's not. It's nonspecific and out of sequence. The glove or target must come *after* the pitch choice. Actually, hitting the glove comes last. First it's the pitch choice and then physical projection, followed by physical implementation. Coach and pitcher must give proper sequencing to pitch selection and pitch location. Concentrating out of this sequence sends mixed messages to the body's nerves and muscles. The fix instruction impedes the fix even with maximal effort. Strikes happen last, the desired result of a properly programmed chain of event.

Let's go through the managed interaction of mind, body, and task. It's basically a four-step learning process, followed by a visualization process, and then followed by a centering process. Again, sequencing is as important to concentration as sequential muscle loading is to mechanics.

LEARNING CONCENTRATION

To learn, a pitcher must (1) take information and instruction from a coach and (2) experience it in competition to acquire (3) intrapersonal and interpersonal knowledge. With this knowledge comes (4) awareness—an awareness of what can go right and an awareness of what can go wrong. Pitchers cannot be taught experience; every pitcher processes experience in competition differently, and level of awareness needs only to support the base of talent and skill at the level of competition at which the athlete should (ideally) succeed. The term overachiever is usually applied to a player who is short on physical tools and long on mental and emotional tools. He has mastered information and instruction, experience, knowledge of self and others, and the awareness of what he has to do right in competition. He's learned what it takes for him, personally, to be successful. Conversely, there's the underachieving player. This is the guy blessed with physical tools who cannot seem to put performance together with any consistency in competition. He can't learn what it takes for him, personally, to be successful. These two profiles represent the bookends of our athletic gene pool. Most pitchers fall somewhere in between with their mental and emotional makeup. All pitchers, however, can be taught and can learn the process of concentration. Once accomplished, visualization can be added to the mix.

All pitchers can learn how to concentrate. Here Troy Percival locks in his target as he prepares to launch.

USING VISUALIZATION TO CONCENTRATE

Visualization is the conscious focusing of an experienced knowledge and awareness base, the mind directing the body toward what can go right. It's important to note that (1) a pitcher's body cannot edit a good or bad visualization; *it implements only;* and (2) a pitcher's body cannot implement even good visualization unless it has *experienced* the visualization with *similar psycho-neuro-immunological intensity*. When adrenaline is flowing at levels beyond what the brain is telling nerves and muscles to do, nerves and muscles will revert to old form.

For a pitcher to do what he did in the bullpen means nothing until he matches up that practice movement with game blood chemistry. Coaches and pitchers should know about this disparity, as should sports psychologists, who unwittingly set up frustration and failure when they advise a pitcher to visualize a past performance as preparation for an upcoming performance. It only works if the pitcher's past performance had the same intra-personal intensity as will be experienced in the new performance. When the athlete cannot take practice skills between the lines in competition, baseball people call it "white-line" fever. The athlete continually reverts to old form. It would actually be better to have athletes recall an adrenaline rush from a past event (a near fall, an almost car wreck) and apply *that* feeling to this pitching performance! Let's go back to the introduction of part III and our computer hardware and software analogy. Applying it to a pitcher with white-line fever, the power surge of competitive adrenaline overloads the relationship between floppy disk and hard-drive capacity. Until there is parity, there can't be optimal performance, and parity only comes with experience. It is a catch-22, so when consciously focusing knowledge and awareness to enhance performance (1) visualize based on experience, (2) keep pushing the envelope of preparation and competition, and (3) be patient until the process matches up. When it does, coach and pitcher are ready for centering.

Centering becomes an athlete's ultimate level of concentration. It combines task-specific visualization with a positive interaction between the conscious and subconscious mind. Let me digress a moment to talk about the conscious and subconscious. The conscious mind is capable of one concrete thought at a time. It gives direction to the subconscious mind that processes 100 million bytes of information per second, the equivalent of two complete volumes of the *Encyclopedia Britannica* every second! Obviously, the subconscious can be a very powerful resource if used properly. Proper use means positive input and direction from the conscious, because the subconscious processes but does not edit. A negative or neutral thought from the conscious mind gets the same dedication as a positive thought, and negative or neutral in competition means failure. I've included written material on centering by Dr. Bill Harrison at the end of this chapter. He's one of the best in sports at explaining the process.

Earlier in this book I mentioned "this pitch, this moment." I also mentioned "there's stuff to process before a pitch, there's the pitch, and then there's stuff to process after the pitch." Centering to a pitcher in competition means consciously processing the before and after, to arrive at a consensus with the subconscious. Centering to a pitcher means a total mental and physical commitment to the task of one pitch, one location. Anything that impedes task-specific visualization is filtered out.

VISUALIZING SUCCESS

One of the best mental training drills is to recall and review in the mind a series of past successes. Compare successes with failures and determine what goes into a consistently good pitching performance.

Try the following visualization exercise:

Close your eyes and reflect upon a particular day when you pitched exceptionally well. Think of specific games or perhaps innings or hitters you pitched to effectively. Think of the time you had good control, command of your pitches, and felt strong emotions. Take considerable time to think about all your pitching successes. Even if you haven't had much success in game situations, think about instances in the bullpen when you had command of your pitches. If you have to think back a few years, in a lower level of ball, think about the times that you were truly in command on the mound.

After reflecting on those top performances, answer "true" or "false" to the following statements:

1. You had a clear idea in the form of a visual picture of exactly how you were going to throw each pitch.   **T** **F**

2. Your concentration was on the task at hand—throwing the ball to the target.   **T** **F**

3. You weren't thinking about making your body or parts of it go through the pitching motion—you just did it.   **T** **F**

4. You were highly aware of seeing your target but the hitters and everything else were just a faint blur.   **T** **F**

5. Your mind was out of your body, as if it were following the ball into the target.   **T** **F**

6. There were no distractions.   **T** **F**

7. Time slowed down. You had plenty of time to think or do what you wanted.   **T** **F**

After you have vividly thought of your successes and responded to the seven questions, examine your reactions:

How do you mentally and physically feel at this moment? Where would your confidence level be if you had the opportunity to go out and pitch right now? I expect you have that good feeling, that high level of confidence. The emotions that you have at this moment are a result of utilizing your mind effectively by visualizing your success. Many of the answers for your success lie within you, within your mind, but you must use your mind properly to obtain the answers.

(continued)

Although I advocate a positive mental approach and believe pitchers learn from their successes, it can also be helpful to analyze our failure. Just don't take it too far. Unfortunately, many pitchers and coaches spend an incredible amount of time and energy searching for the whys of poor performance. That's negative.

Good, accurate feedback is necessary for improving and learning, in pitching or in any other sports performance. When feedback is accurate, even of a subpar performance, it can be the information that gets you over the hump.

Consider the simple game of darts. How would you perform at darts if you were blindfolded? Perhaps you could execute good mechanics and fundamentals and fire the dart toward a target. But if there was no feedback about how close you were to the target or how far you missed, how would you plan your next toss? Think about it. Do you think you would get more consistently accurate tossing the dart even if you had 100 tosses? No, it wouldn't matter how much you drilled on mechanics and fundamentals. Your performance and consistency would probably not improve because you had no mental game plan, no specific target, and no feedback.

When a proper mental game plan has been developed, then drilling on mechanics and fundamentals can be very useful. Remember Fernando Valenzuela looking at the sky during his delivery? How about the free throw Michael Jordan sank with his eyes closed on national TV? Both these athletes could perform their skill without looking because they had done it eyes open, with perfect mechanics, countless times in practice. They had already programmed the feedback of mechanics, inner feelings, and a proper mental approach.

Reflect upon some of your poorer pitching performances. Again vividly visualizing the game situations, the teams, the weather conditions, the crowd, emotions, how your body felt, and so on. Think of various games, hitters, and specific innings. Now answer "true" or "false" to the following statements:

1. You did not have a clear idea in the form of a visual picture of exactly what you wanted to do with each pitch and how you wanted to throw it.   **T** **F**

2. You thought a lot about what you didn't want to do, like walking a batter, not hanging a curve ball, not wasting a pitch too far outside, and so on.   **T** **F**

3. You were highly aware of some part of your body, as if you were steering that part of the body through the motion.   **T** **F**

4. Your concentration was on previous pitches or situations, or future pitches or situations, or on things totally unrelated to the game.   **T** **F**

(continued)

124

5. You cannot recall seeing your target at the time you were into your motion or throwing the pitch.　　　　　T　F

6. You can recall distraction(s).　　　　　T　F

Examine your reactions. If you answered "false" to most of the questions when you were pitching successfully and "true" when you were pitching poorly, you are like most athletes.

Consistently successful performers control their concentration. They use visualization, a heightened awareness of what the eyes are seeing, and control of their physical energy, so that the body just reacts with good rhythm and timing. Visual-mental skills can be learned just as easily as the ability to hit, run, or throw various types of pitches. The more you put into it, the more you will get out of it.

The fundamentals of visualization must be worked on and refined constantly. But it pays off in big dividends. Many talented pitchers with strong arms never achieve consistently good performance. Start visualizing yourself visualizing and self-fulfill your prophecy!

Consistently successful performers, such as Pedro Martinez, control their concentration as well as their physical energy. The body reacts with good rhythm and timing.

CENTERING

Bill Harrison, OD, AAO

Many pitchers have had great success in learning to control their concentration by controlling a physical process we call "centering." Centering is what concentration is all about.

To illustrate how centering works, tune into the background noises around you. Perhaps someone is talking, a baby is crying, a bird is chirping, there are street noises in the distance, or perhaps there is the hum of an air conditioner. Now shift your attention to your sleeves. Take time. As you are shifting your centering to your clothing, what happened to the background sounds? Did they fade for an instant? Notice as you center in on one system the other tends to fade into the background. This process of selective attention is called centering.

Do you ever drive down the highway and suddenly realize that you missed your turnoff miles back? Do you ever read to the bottom of the page and nothing registers? There are times when a pitcher is looking at the catcher, but his mind has drifted to something completely off the baseball field. He was still centering, but not on the task at hand, and that resulted in poor concentration. The point is, we are always centering.

Any of you can center on a thought, something you see, hear, touch, feel, taste, or smell, but you can center on only one thing at a given time. Of course, you can shift your centering so fast from one thing to another that it seems as though you are paying attention to more than one thing at a time, but that is very similar to watching television for an hour but changing channels every five seconds. At the end of the hour you could safely say that you expended a lot of energy watching television, you tried hard, you were bearing down, but nothing registered.

Focusing in the Present

When you pitch at your peak, you probably recall that it was as if your mind was in the present. That is, you centered only on what was happening at the time. You did not think about prior plays, situations, or future concerns. Between hitters, when the action stopped, you may have shifted your attention to something relaxing: the clouds overhead, a tree in the distance, or even a fan in the stands. But once the hitter was in the box, your attention was totally on getting the job done.

Learning to control that skill can aid in maintaining concentration in the here and now, no matter what the conditions of the game may be. Not only must you pitch in the proper time and space, you must center in the proper degree. You can center widely, taking in as much information as possible, or you can "fine center," in which case your attention is channeled into a very small area. For example, an effective fine center for a pitcher would be to direct his centering to the webbing in the catcher's glove, or a scratch on his knee guard, or the stitching or insignia on his sleeve. When you center on a target with your eyes, everything else blurs and fades away.

When you center widely, called "space centering," you're literally spacing out. Your mind drifts and is rarely on one thing for any length of time.

This translates to other sports. Most athletes are more accurate in their kicking, throwing, hitting, or touching when they have been fine centered on a target. There is no right way to do it. But, as mentioned previously, the answers lie within each individual.

Relate to your past successes. What was the degree of centering when you were most consistently successful? What was your target? To have the kind of concentration necessary to be a consistently top performer, you must not only learn how to stay centered on your target but also be able to accurately determine the proper target.

Target Selection

Target selection can be simplified if you ask yourself, "What is my job as a pitcher?" Most pitchers tell me that their job is winning, striking out the hitter, not giving up any runs, and so forth. But those are really goals, desirable ones, but not the target for our centering. No matter what the condition may be at any given time, including the score and even the importance of a particular hitter, the pitcher's job is always the same. Whether it is Little League tryouts or the seventh game of the World Series, the pitcher must throw the ball to a target. That target may be the catcher's glove, his mask, his knee guard, or it may be a visual zone over home plate.

In the bullpen warming up or in workouts between games or spring training, it is a totally different situation. If you or your coach determines that you need work on a position, for example, then you had better be centered exclusively on the body awareness system.

Your criterion of success should be whether you execute the shoulder turn properly, not whether you threw the ball to the target. In fact, I find that when most pitchers say they are working on mechanics, they think about the mechanics they are going to focus on, but when they go into the motion and release the ball, they are not centering on the specific fundamentals, but are just space centering generally on what they feel and the target they see. The result is the "grooving" of poor mechanics. It is very important that the pitcher works on mechanics and fundamentals, so when he needs to perform the skill in a game situation, he's able to do it successfully. Isolate a specific fundamental and center on it. Don't be concerned with the accuracy or quality of the pitch. Even if you throw the ball over the backstop, a properly executed fundamental will ultimately help your effectiveness. The task at hand? To center on the fundamental and develop it so that it becomes a proper and natural reaction.

When centering is on one specific part of the body, the rest of the body will not flow with proper rhythm and timing. That particular fundamental movement improves. The results of the efforts are not judged by the ability to throw strikes when centering on the mechanics. Rather, they are judged by the ability to throw quality pitches to a target when on the mound during a game and allowing the body to react. If it doesn't react with good mechanics, return to the bullpen for more specific attention to fundamentals. You must specifically center on them, but your practice session must include specific attention on the mental game plan you're going to use in the same situation next time out.

In the bullpen, you must practice centering on different targets. Determine if you get better results by looking at the target at all times, from the beginning to the end of the delivery, or if you are better off with spot centering on the target, looking away during part of your motion, and then looking back at the target just before delivery. Perhaps what works best for you at one time may be slightly different as your expertise and concentration skills increase.

You must develop a game plan. Although the score and the situation vary, you need a game plan to stay tuned to each individual element. After all, in game conditions your job is always the same—throw the ball to a target. That task never varies despite the score or playing conditions. Therefore, you need a consistent plan to follow, one that is workable during all conditions: when you feel strong or weak, up or down, and whether you are winning or losing.

A Centering Plan

Here is a plan that will help you develop consistency in your approach to the game. You will find that you will get more out of your workouts and learn more from your game experiences. Like all physical performances, this approach will only reach its potential with a certain amount of practice. Once developed properly, through practice, this approach will become reflex and natural and will be an automatic way of approaching the game. Before each pitch, go through the following steps:

1. Analyze the situation: This step is straightforward, but if it is not incorporated into the game plane, you are doomed for inconsistency. During this step, survey the game situation, the score, the count, the outs, and the base runners, and analyze the hitter. Determine the best pitch that you can make at this time, but think about what the batter is likely to be looking for before making the final pitch selection. Think about fielding situations that you may have to react to. Part of this step takes place before the catcher gives the sign and part of it after the pitch is selected.

2. Visualize and energize the pitch: Experiment in the bullpen and learn from game situations how to use this step most effectively. The minimum would be to visualize the last 15 to 20 feet of the pitch you expect to throw and literally see it in its final trajectory. The quality of this visualization will have a direct impact on the value of this step, so attempt to visualize clearly including visualizing the spin of the particular pitch. With experience, it will be possible to visualize the complete pitching motion, with proper mechanics and the great feeling of a flow of energy through the body. The visualization of the pitching motion will then flow into the trajectory of the pitch going all the way to the target.

3. Fine center on the target: Pinpoint centering on the smallest target possible. Fine centering does not mean tightening or aiming the ball. Even though you are fine centering with your mind, let your body flow to the target. It will seem as though you are connected to the target by an invisible funnel, and as the pitch is released you are so centered that you will follow the ball right into the target. It is as if your centering directs and controls all your energies.

4. Execute: Proper execution is a product of having the basic skills, the knowledge of the fundamentals and techniques, visualization of the desired performance, and centering on the target.

5. Play back: This, without doubt, is the most important step to master in becoming a consistent top performer. After each pitch, determine whether you analyzed, visualized, and centered properly. It takes more than having good intentions. Do it! Develop the habit after each pitch, particularly in the bullpen, to visualize from start to finish the previous pitch. In visualizing the previous pitch, play back the quality and accuracy of your prepitch visualization and you will play back specifically what you centered on during the pitch. From this point, you will know concretely what you must continue centering on to get the best results, and if there was breakdown in your centering control, those factors that led to a physical or fundamental mistake. Often, the reason performance broke down was improper centering. By adjusting centering, you can get back to the execution of proper fundamentals with the next pitch.

HOUSE RULES

We've all heard or read about players who get "in the zone" during competition. They get locked into a successful performance by managing mind, body, and task: the process of concentration. *It can be taught; it can be learned.*

- Manage the process in sequence: see the required action, feel the required action, do the required action.
- Commit to the process in preparation and competition . . . every throw, every pitch.

See it, feel it, do it!

OK, now that we've discussed pitching with concentration, let's move to chapter 10 and figure out how to pitch with confidence.

CHAPTER 10

Confidence

"Confidence comes not so much from winning
as it does from not being afraid to lose!"

Confidence is an intangible feeling that is usually preceded by preparation and followed by success. The operative word here is *feeling*. A pitcher doesn't think confidence, he feels confidence. A pitcher who prepares properly always feels more confident about his chances of succeeding in competition than a pitcher who hasn't prepared properly. In baseball, because it's a game of failure, confidence is a huge emotional tool both to defend and enhance an athlete's competitive makeup. As you can tell, in all my books and videos, and clinics and consults, I inform and instruct in steps, sequencing from the most basic to the most complex, in order of importance. I'll do the same in this chapter. The foundations of confidence are laid out for you as follows: (1) preparation for performance, (2) competition and performance, (3) success from performance. The synergy from 1 and 3 support confidence in 2, but all are of equal importance to a confident pitcher.

GAINING CONFIDENCE

There are four parts to integrate when preparing for performance: (a) mental conditioning, (b) physical conditioning, (c) nutritional conditioning, and (d) skill conditioning. The effort exerted on an individual part depends on each pitcher's composite of talent and skill. Common sense dictates that the shorter on talent a player is, the harder he must prepare to develop skills to support performance in competition. The point is that at the higher levels of competition, if a pitcher has left himself short in any part of preparation, then he might get lucky or might look cocky (false confidence), but he will never be truly confident. No amount of superstition, no amount of prayer, absolutely nothing will compensate for lack of preparation. (Even the Bible says the Lord helps those who help themselves!)

Responsibility for the preparation that builds confidence must fall on the *player's* shoulders. Accountability can come from his coach, interpersonally, or his competitive result, intrapersonally. Pitcher and coach must know responsibility and accountability go hand in hand, the precursor to both trying and competing. No matter how good a coach is, the pitcher must take preparation between the lines to win or lose accordingly. With competition and performance, it's pretty straightforward. Anybody can try to compete, but it's performing in competition, beating the opposition, getting the job done, that separate winners from losers at every level. Baseball is Darwinian; if you don't win, you lose. If you lose too much, you're out of the game. I need to expand a bit on *trying* versus *doing* in competition. There are too many players out there who have only been made responsible and held accountable for trying hard. Coaches and parents haven't educated their athletes to understand that just to try hard isn't enough, that there are no entitlements.

To get a scholarship or to get a professional contract, trying is only a start; a player must have *success* in competition. Now don't misunderstand my message. I'm not saying a 12-year-old has to compete like a 22-year-old. Let the Little Leaguer play, let him try, let him learn, let him have fun. I am saying that when a youngster understands a scholarship or a signing bonus, when he's ready to commit, then he's ready to compete. If you want a time frame for this choice, it's usually sophomore or junior year in high school when the youngsters can handle the decision.

Curt Schilling's confidence comes in part from his preparation prior to competition. A pitcher who prepares properly feels more confident about his chances of success than a pitcher who hasn't prepared properly.

Now, as I mentioned in the first paragraph of this chapter, preparation builds confidence to compete, success in competition reinforces the feeling of confidence, and a successful performance is both a public and personal confidence builder. They feed on one another. And one last call on confidence: The whole process of preparation, competition, and success works wonders for an athlete's substance and character—not just in baseball but in life.

HOUSE RULES

For coach and player, seek the right information and the right instruction to ensure the right preparation. Always ask, "Why was I successful?" or, "Why wasn't I successful?" If you don't have the right answer, keep looking until you find it.

For coach and player, know with confidence that the right preparation will more often yield the right result in competition. Anything else makes baseball a game of chance, and there's no confidence in chance.

Don't just do it, do it right!

Now that confidence has been defined and discussed and you know it's a teachable feeling for pitchers at any level of competition, you're ready to move on to another important tool for building mental toughness and establishing emotional balance on the mound: self-direction.

CHAPTER 11

Self-Direction

"Having lost sight of my objective,
I doubled my efforts to get there and got nowhere."

Of all the chapters in this book, this chapter can most obviously tip the scales in favor of or against most athletes. Based on 32 years of professional baseball experience, as well as 5 years of clinical and 25 years of academic research, I've found that unless a player self-directs, he just doesn't survive in baseball. Self- direction has as many interpretations and applications as there are athletic skills and personalities, but there are also common threads. In previous chapters we informed and instructed. We also placed responsibility and accountability where it belongs, directly on the individual athlete. Now we glue all of it together by detailing some of the processes that make a player self-directed. I've observed these processes in every successful pitcher I've worked with, no matter his race, economic background, intelligence, or age. Let's begin by laying a foundation for self-direction.

HELPING YOURSELF THROUGH SELF-AWARENESS

Athletes must know themselves to help themselves. There are actually four levels of self-awareness that every pitcher must go through as a function of his talent and skill, his information and experience, and his competition and performance level:

1. Unconscious incompetent (knows nothing and can't do anything)
2. Conscious incompetent (knows something but can't do anything with it)
3. Unconscious competent (knows little, if anything, but does it anyway)
4. Conscious competent (knows what he needs to know and is successful doing it)

Obviously, number 4 is where everybody would eventually like to be. Number 3 will work until the player starts failing too much; then he doesn't know how to fix the failure. Number 2 is usually a talent and skill problem resulting in a short career, and obviously number 1 is entry-level baseball.

To have self-awareness requires objective self-assessment. By looking at the above four levels for a point-in-time assessment you can determine where you currently are. If where you are isn't where you want to be, define where you want to be and connect the dots. It will focus mind and body and make your preparation a lot more efficient.

By defining an objective or series of objectives, you won't work hard going nowhere. Assessing where you are can be emotionally upsetting—a wake-up call to reality. Don't let this impede self-improvement or self-direction.

Understanding self-emotion is a prerequisite to self-awareness and self-direction. Optimal levels of emotion are managed, not controlled. Anger, elation, aggressiveness, fear, anxiety, and insecurity are normal emotions. They are also acceptable in baseball if appropriately vented at the appropriate time and place and for the appropriate reason. Successful veterans will experience the same intense emotions in competition as hotheaded rookies, but they've learned to manage them properly. Veterans seldom let emotion get in the way of competition. Self-emotion management can be learned, and it can become an important coping tool for successes and failures on and off the baseball playing field.

Few players have trouble with an objective. Success and failure in competition—wins and losses, strikes and balls, hits and strikeouts and walks—are external benchmarks. It's the feeling that goes with success and failure in competition that causes most of the problems, because it is internal and unique to the player. This feeling is processed psychologically, neurologically, and immunologically, and will elicit a fight-flee-freeze response in the body. Emotions are subsets of these responses. All of these feelings and emotions are normal, and they will happen (any one, or in combination) pitch to pitch, inning to inning, game to game, season to season. Embrace them, work them, manage them, just don't let them impede preparation or performance.

Managing your motivation is also important to self-direction, self-awareness, and self-assessment. Remember that baseball is a game of failure. Anyone can stay motivated when things go well. But you should know going in that because of failure, motivation in baseball requires persistence. Figure out quickly what keeps your motivation muscles strong, because only the persistent survive in baseball.

USING AFFIRMATIONS TO SUCCEED

Affirm your self-direction, self-awareness, self-emotion management, and self-motivation management. Affirmations are positive statements to self about self or task. They match up conscious and subconscious mind with body and performance. There are millions of possible affirmations. The Bible is full of them. In House Rules on the next page, I give some real-life affirmations. The best ones I've found for baseball are (1) generic, such as "I can do this" or "Yes, I can," which sends a positive "warm fuzzy" to total body in any situation, or (2) a combination of generic with specific task, such as "I can do this (workout)," or "Yes, I can" (throw this curveball down and away for a strike), which sends the total body a positive message specific to the situation at hand. Affirmations repeated in large numbers work to overcome many of the negatives in a game of failure.

"Fake it until you make it" with self-awareness and self-emotion management. Only you know how nervous, angry, or scared you are. Many times, appearing to be in control gives you control.

To stay motivated, find a routine that works for you; avoid ritual. By definition in a routine, you control your choices; in a ritual, it controls you. Rituals will lead to monotonous overtraining or neural stagnation—self defeat!

It looks pretty simple on paper, but it's not. And it never becomes easy because of the uncontrollable variables involved in competition on the mound. With practice, however, you can teach yourself to direct your mind and body toward addressing only the controllable variables of the task at hand.

HOUSE RULES

Use the following affirmations before every important baseball decision:

- Ask yourself these questions: What ought to be done for me? Will it injure me or others? Is this in accord with my beliefs and goals? Is it in alignment with reality as I see it? Am I willing to fully accept the consequences?

- To be truly successful in the game and to grow in self-esteem, I must not give up my growth, pursuit of fulfillment, or happiness to anyone.

- I choose to treat myself with dignity and move toward success in baseball with passion, wisdom, freedom, and joy for the game. I am the authority over me.

- To release my competitive potential from past restrictive programming of my subconscious, it is extremely important that I give myself the right to be me and to function as I choose. It is not possible to have sound self-esteem if I am not true to myself or if I give up responsibility and accountability for my own life as I seek to achieve fulfillment of my needs and goals in baseball.

- I want to allow myself the freedom to choose success in baseball without building a prison for myself with "have to's," "can'ts," and "they won't let me's."

- I recognize I am functioning from my own free choice and I can either recognize myself as important, valuable, and interesting, or see myself as an absolute incompetent who is unworthy and unneeded. I can choose to be kind, caring, helpful, loyal, and compassionate, or to be lazy, cowardly, mean, and disloyal. I can choose to be happy, free, and to succeed as a pitcher, or to fail and feel unimportant and less than others.

- If I allow myself this freedom in baseball, I must recognize I am responsible for my decisions and actions and be willing to accept the consequences they bring.

- I know I am the one who will answer for my every action and will profit or suffer accordingly.

- Someone else's opinion of me has nothing to do with what I think of myself. Hitters will let me know if I can pitch.

ATHLETIC DESIRE INDEX

The Athletic Desire Index was developed by Dr. Matt Mitchell, a professional tour golfer, one-time member of the Interservices Boxing Team, and creator of "Pre-Sport Focusing" audio tapes, and Dr. Alan Blitzblau as a way to measure the competitive desire of athletes. Both male and female elite athletes, aged 13-49, were used in the development of the test. The Index consists of a questionnaire of 97 questions that relate to different components of competitive desire, such as determination and mental toughness. Once the test is taken and scored, an athlete can determine what components of competitive desire need to be improved. A sample chart showing the seven different components, or subscales, of athletic desire is shown below.

SEVEN SUBSCALES OF ATHLETIC DESIRE

How can you see inside athletes to measure the size of their hearts? This index measures the desire of an athlete to be the best. There are seven subscale measurements that can be used by coaches and athletes themselves to monitor performance issues and allow for personal growth.

The seven subscales measure various areas of desire and give clues to how an athlete may act in stressful situations. A low score in one or more areas suggests there is a need to assist the athlete to overcome those deficits. This may be accomplished by individual coaching skills or it may require the assistance of a sports psychologist to help "reprogram" the athlete's thinking patterns.

For instance, an athlete who rates highly in all the subscales except emotional control can be given psychological assistance to learn to be under pressure in order to maximize performance.

- **Internal Motivation.** How much does the athlete want to sacrifice to win? How were these attitudes implanted historically? Will the athlete be willing to pay the price to reach the top?

- **Drive.** Does the athlete respond positively to competition? Does the athlete aspire to accomplish difficult tasks? Will the athlete willingly set and maintain high goals?

- **Mental Toughness.** Can an athlete accept strong criticism without feeling hurt? Can the athlete bounce back quickly from adversity or bad breaks? Does the athlete need excessive encouragement to maintain standards of performance? Can the athlete handle rough coaching styles? Does the athlete become overly upset with losing or bad performance?

- **Emotional Management.** Is the athlete not easily depressed or frustrated by bad breaks or mistakes? Does the athlete tend to be emotionally stable and realistic about sports? Can the athlete keep feelings during competition to a minimum and not have a performance be affected by them? Will the athlete blow up in competition and cost a win for himself or his team?

- **Self-Confidence.** Does the athlete make decisions confidently or is the athlete indecisive? Are unexpected competitive situations handled well? Does the athlete have unfaltering confidence in himself? Is the athlete confident in his or her skills and abilities?

- **Determination.** Is the athlete willing to persevere, even in the face of great difficulty? Is the athlete unrelenting in work habits? Will the athlete hang in and work out problems or will the athlete give up quickly? Is the athlete willing to practice as long as necessary to achieve the highest possible skill levels?

- **Responsibility.** Does the athlete accept criticism and blame even when it is not deserved? Does the athlete tend to dwell too long on mistakes and indulge in forms of self-punishment for them? Will the athlete take responsibility for decisions rather than relying on the advice of others? Is the athlete willing to endure intense physical, emotional, and mental pain for the sake of self-improvement? Will the athlete play even when injured?

A sample chart showing the results by one elite athlete is shown below. If you have the following questionnaire scored, it will indicate how you perform in each subscale, as well as your areas of strength and areas for improvement.

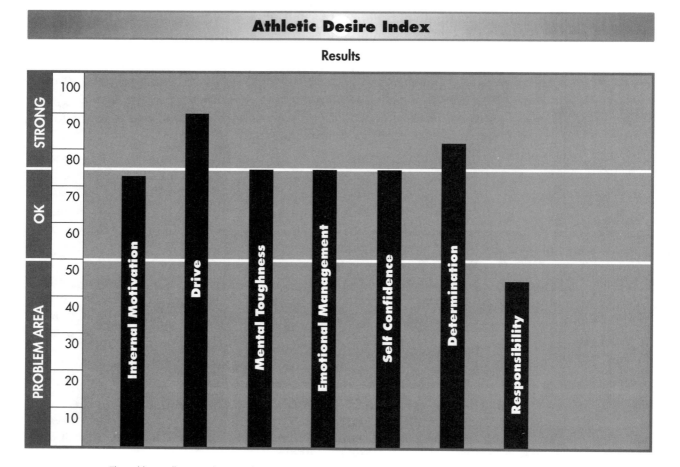

This athlete will respond positively in competitive situations based on the strong Drive score, but will have a continuing tendency to blame all others—coaches, teammates, officials, but never himself—for all failures as registered by the low score in Responsibility. The athlete's coaches and family will have to work diligently to teach him that he has an equal part of any failures which occur. It will be necessary to help him understand the contradictions with his strong Drive. Athletes who score *Strong* in most categories and who have no *Problem Areas* are likely to excel in their sport and have the potential to play professionally.

ATHLETIC DESIRE INDEX QUESTIONNAIRE

The purpose of this questionnaire is to help you learn more about yourself. It is designed to assist you as an athlete to improve your performances. It is necessary to answer all questions. If in doubt, pick the answer that is closest to how you feel. Go with your first reaction, rather than think too long or too hard about a question. There are no right or wrong answers. This is not a timed project, but it is simple and you should be able to conclude it quickly. For information about how to score the test, contact Dr. Alan Blitzblau or Dr. Matt Mitchell at the addresses shown at the end of the test.

Please circle the answer that best fits how you feel.	Always	Usually	Occasionally	Rarely
1. During competition, I give myself pep talks.	A	B	C	D
2. I thought about breaking sports records when I was younger.	A	B	C	D
3. When I do well, I'm disappointed if I'm not praised.	A	B	C	D
4. During competition, I find it hard to control my feelings.	A	B	C	D
5. In my sport, I'm very confident.	A	B	C	D
6. When I start working on a new technique in my sport, I often will work on it to the point of exhaustion.	A	B	C	D
7. I feel responsible when I lose, despite what any other performers may have done.	A	B	C	D
8. I get angry and call myself names when I screw up during competition.	A	B	C	D
9. During practice sessions, I get annoyed when others fool around instead of being serious.	A	B	C	D
10. If I broke training and was questioned about it, I would lie to stay out of trouble.	A	B	C	D
11. I get depressed when I have trouble mastering a technique or skill in my sport.	A	B	C	D
12. I lose hope about winning when a contest is going badly.	A	B	C	D
13. I frequently will practice on my own as well as at regularly scheduled times.	A	B	C	D
14. I can't sleep well at night before a contest because I keep thinking about it and how I will do.	A	B	C	D
15. It is all right to lose if I have given my best possible performance.	A	B	C	D
16. People can always say of me that I will do almost anything to win.	A	B	C	D
17. I think I am more sensitive than most athletes.	A	B	C	D
18. It is hard for me not to be affected throughout a contest if I make an early mistake.	A	B	C	D
19. Sometimes, I screw up during a contest because I can't make up my mind quickly enough.	A	B	C	D
20. I get tired just thinking about a long, hard practice.	A	B	C	D

		Always	Usually	Occasionally	Rarely
21.	I know some athletes who have been successful without working very hard.	A	B	C	D
22.	If I have a bad performance and still win, it is not really okay.	A	B	C	D
23.	I try harder in competition than I do in practice.	A	B	C	D
24.	I never worry about getting injured.	A	B	C	D
25.	I get discouraged when there are several bad breaks during competition.	A	B	C	D
26.	I usually handle unexpected situations during competition very well.	A	B	C	D
27.	Sometimes during breaks in practice sessions, I find myself daydreaming.	A	B	C	D
28.	Working out is meaningful only when done to a point of really hurting as in "no pain, no gain."	A	B	C	D
29.	I am always a "graceful" or "good" loser.	A	B	C	D
30.	It is important to me to be considered one of the most emotionally tough competitors by fellow athletes.	A	B	C	D
31.	I feel sometimes that I'm not as good as some of my fellow competitors.	A	B	C	D
32.	I can understand athletes who think that being liked by their coach is more important than doing a really good job.	A	B	C	D
33.	I like the "pressure" of competition best about my sport.	A	B	C	D
34.	Long hours of hard practice is the most important part of becoming a successful athlete.	A	B	C	D
35.	My mistakes sometimes really bother me for days.	A	B	C	D
36.	I wish I could stay home more instead of having to travel so much.	A	B	C	D
37.	Hustle is really important, but it doesn't make up for a lack of basic talent.	A	B	C	D
38.	I feel a good chewing out can help athletes perform better.	A	B	C	D
39.	I have trouble putting small problems and disagreements out of my mind during practice or competition.	A	B	C	D
40.	When I face really great athletes I feel humble and scared.	A	B	C	D
41.	There are some drills and practice exercises that I have trouble sticking to.	A	B	C	D
42.	Even when my coach criticizes me unfairly, I still feel guilty.	A	B	C	D
43.	Sometimes, when things are going bad during competition, I forget important "keys" to good performance.	A	B	C	D
44.	Most of my fellow athletes tell me I'm a really hard worker.	A	B	C	D
45.	The coaches I have played best for were tough and hard-nosed.	A	B	C	D
46.	Losing really scares me.	A	B	C	D

	Always	Usually	Occasionally	Rarely
47. I think I can become one of the best in my sport.	A	B	C	D
48. I am willing to practice longer and harder than most of my fellow athletes.	A	B	C	D
49. I think my coaches criticize me sometimes without good reasons.	A	B	C	D
50. Sometimes it is all right to have a couple of drinks or a little bit of drugs because I'll sweat it out the next day.	A	B	C	D
51. My mother used to get on me when I first started in my sport because I didn't play well enough.	A	B	C	D
52. I imagine there will always be someone better than me in my sport.	A	B	C	D
53. To succeed, I need the encouragement of my coach.	A	B	C	D
54. The weather seldom affects my feelings during competition.	A	B	C	D
55. I feel I'm not quite as good as some of my fellow competitors.	A	B	C	D
56. I practice only as hard as necessary to get by although to others it looks like I'm really working hard.	A	B	C	D
57. I usually perform best without the advice of others.	A	B	C	D
58. When I win, it means I'm a really good person.	A	B	C	D
59. When I didn't do well in sports when I was young, my father would get really upset with me.	A	B	C	D
60. I get disgusted with myself when I haven't learned a skill properly.	A	B	C	D
61. I believe things go on with my fellow competitors that I don't know about.	A	B	C	D
62. Even when I'm looking forward to competition, I don't always feel ready for it when the time comes.	A	B	C	D
63. I believe I have a great deal of self-confidence in my sport.	A	B	C	D
64. Doing interviews and signing autographs really bug me.	A	B	C	D
65. Once I try something in my sport, I work on it until I've got it down perfectly.	A	B	C	D
66. I will keep playing when injured even though most others would quit if they had the same injury.	A	B	C	D
67. I'll sacrifice everything to be the best in my sport.	A	B	C	D
68. My teachers praised me only when I performed well in sports.	A	B	C	D
69. I think an athlete should take it easy on a competitor who obviously is not as good.	A	B	C	D
70. I often perform poorly after being severely criticized by a coach, the fans, or the media.	A	B	C	D
71. I feel the life of an athlete has too many restrictions and frustrations.	A	B	C	D
72. Sometimes, I feel I don't have the ability to do all the things I want to in my sport.	A	B	C	D

73. After a long, hard practice, I usually think about the mistakes I made.   A   B   C   D

74. I usually compete best without the advice of others.   A   B   C   D

75. No matter what reasons, I hate myself as a failure when I lose.   A   B   C   D

76. My coaches ridiculed me a lot when I was just starting out in sports.   A   B   C   D

77. I keep practicing hard even when others are just fooling around.   A   B   C   D

78. I often lose my temper in competition.   A   B   C   D

79. I never make any excuse when I get caught violating training rules.   A   B   C   D

80. When things are going badly in competition, I think I can change them for the better.   A   B   C   D

81. It's not my fault if I lose in competition but have done my best and others have screwed up.   A   B   C   D

82. After a hard practice, I seldom try to work out some more.   A   B   C   D

83. I never lose hope that I can win even when a competition is going badly.   A   B   C   D

84. Working hard enough to cause pain is an important part of becoming a winner.   A   B   C   D

85. My family and friends have always treated me as special because I am a good athlete.   A   B   C   D

86. It is terrible to lose, no matter what the circumstances, even when I have given my best performance.   A   B   C   D

87. I always wanted to become a professional athlete.   A   B   C   D

88. I believe that pain, torture, and agony are part of the price to pay to become a winner.   A   B   C   D

89. I often get excited knowing I've got a long, hard practice coming up.   A   B   C   D

90. Winning in competition is more important than the amount of money that can be earned.   A   B   C   D

91. I don't let some bad breaks in competition get me down.   A   B   C   D

92. Reporters are always making a lot of stupid mistakes.   A   B   C   D

93. Talent is really important, but I'd rather be known for my good attitude and hustle.   A   B   C   D

94. If I had a possible career-ending injury and was unable to get into the best championship in my sport (World Series, Super Bowl, U.S. Open, etc.), I'd play regardless of the future.   A   B   C   D

95. Being a champion has too many public responsibilities.   A   B   C   D

96. I believe it is important for me to motivate myself rather than rely on others for motivation and encouragement.   A   B   C   D

97. I love to be up against the best athletes because of the challenge to do as well as them.   A   B   C   D

For information about how to score this test, please contact:

Dr. Alan Blitzblau
104 Mill View Circle
Williamsburg, VA 23185
e-mail: alan@alcon-rehab.com

Or

Dr. Matt Mitchell
9760 Caminito Doha
San Diego, CA 92131
(858) 536-9725
e-mail: drmattym@access1.net

For other information, go to www.tomhouse.com.

CONCLUSION

So now you and your pitcher have a game plan. Is it the final answer to pitchers and coaches? Heck no! But it's the best we have *at this point in time*. As long as I continue to find better ways to teach something old, or discover new information and instruction protocols to improve the way we teach pitchers, I'll stay visible and vocal, and will continue to develop and refine my methods.

My challenge to you? Don't be afraid to change your paradigm—get out of the box! Nobody has been more wrong, or right, about preparing pitchers than I have. Don't let ego get in the way of good sense. Good intentions are nice, but good information, instruction, and inspiration are necessary. And remember, although winning is important, no one can control who wins. A pitcher can only control himself and make certain he gives the best he has. The best will likely lead to winning, or at least keep him in the game and give him a chance to win. Pitching skill is not an accident of birth. It can be developed through training. This approach promises no miracles, but it can help pitchers approach the peak of their individual performances, and give them *the pitching edge.*

INDEX

pitches, *cont.*
  velocity 46
plyometric exercises 70-71
postural stabilization 14-21
  drills for *18-19*
practice throwing 104-106
preparation 109, 110-111, 132-134
proprioception 2

R

recovery 64, 65, *66-68*
release point 41
relief pitchers, microcycle 69
resistance training 54, 55, 60-65, 96, 106
Righetti, Dave *51*
Rijo, Jose *51*
rotator-cuff injuries 101
rubber 17
rushing 6
Ryan, Nolan 6, 15, 57, 65, 114

S

scouting reports 115
screwball
  grip 45
  release *42*
Seaver, Tom *11*
self-awareness 120, 136-139
self-direction 136-139
shoulders 24, 100
side lunges 80
side step-downs 81
side-ups 78
sinker grip 44
sit-ups 81-86
skill training 55
slider grip 44
split finger grip 44
sprints 71
stamina 56, 70-71
step drill *9*
step-ups 81
Stewart, Dave *29*
stick figures, explained 3
straight-leg wall sit-ups 82
strategy, pitching 114-117

strength 24
  building *vs.* maintaining 61-62
  devising training program 63, 100-101
  functional 53-54
  preventing injuries with balanced 99-101
  vs. endurance 61, 69-70
stretch *vs.* windup 14, 21
stride 16-17
subconscious mind 122
success 110-111, 137
visualizing 123-125
Sutcliffe, Rick *29*

T

target, centering on 126-128
throwing, practice 104-105
thumbs-up, thumbs-down pull 95
torque chart *94*
torso flexes 75
torso rotation 100
  drills for *35*
  late 32-36
towel drill with partner *18-19,* 34
training
  annual schedule 54-55
  bodywork 70, 77-86, *98*
  emphasis of 69-70
  flexibility 69, 70, 71-76
  overview 64-65
  principles 64-65, 70
  stamina 56, 70-71
  volumes 62, 64
trunk stabilization 81-86
two knee drill *49*

U

underachievers 120
underloading 63
upper body
  spine-to-hip relationship 16
  strength training 62

V

velocity, pitch 46
video technology 1, 2, 98-99

149

Viola, Frank *11*
visualization 110, 111, 121-125

W

wall crunches 82
weight training 53, 60
weight transfer 26
"white-line" fever 122

why me's 96
wide-stance leg flexes 74
windup 14, 21
working the count 116-117
wrists 38

Y

yearly training schedule 54-55

ABOUT THE AUTHOR

Tom House is one of the top pitching experts in the world. After playing for the legendary Rod Dedeaux at USC, House pitched in the Major Leagues for the Atlanta Braves from 1967 to 1975, for the Boston Red Sox from 1976 to 1977, and for the Seattle Mariners from 1977 to 1979. He then coached pitchers for the Houston Astros, San Diego Padres, and Texas Rangers. He also has coached in Japan and Latin America.

In addition to his on-field experience, House has made pitching a scientific study. His company, Bio-Kinetics, uses computer-generated, three-dimensional motion analysis to help athletes maximize performance through proper biomechanics. House also holds a PhD in psychology and has been a sport psychology consultant for many professional and amateur baseball players.

House is the author of eight previous books on baseball and has produced eight instructional videos on pitching. He is a member of the Major League Baseball Players' Association, as well as the American College of Sports Medicine and the Association for the Advancement of Applied Sport Psychology. In 1998 House was presented with the American Baseball Coaches Association's lifetime achievement award.

When he's not coaching or analyzing pitchers, House enjoys jogging, weight training, and golf. He and his wife, Marie, live in Del Mar, California.

Add skill & power
to your game

This video shows how pitching technique is taught, performed, and corrected for maximum efficiency and effectiveness on the mound. Featuring former major league pitcher and top pitching coach Tom House, *The Pitching Edge Video* combines practical on-field instruction and drills with expert off-field analysis and explanation. You'll benefit from the many flat-ground and mound practice drills presented; and you'll gain insight into common problems and how to overcome them through Coach House's slow-motion video analysis of each phase of the pitching motion.

(54-minute video) • ISBN 0-87322-787-5

In *Fit To Pitch*, pitching guru Tom House combines his on-field experiences, weight-room workouts, and years of research to deliver proven, practical applications that will strengthen anyone's pitching throughout the year. Outlined within are essential training components to develop more speed, strength, and stamina on the mound; pitcher-specific workouts for year-round conditioning; and rehabilitation guidelines that help players return to competition faster and more safely.

216 pages • ISBN 0-87322-882-0

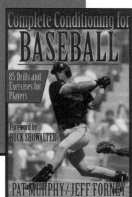

Complete Conditioning for Baseball is the training guide you need for more power and speed. Arizona State University's baseball coach, Pat Murphy, and the Arizona Diamondback's strength and conditioning coach, Jeff Forney, share the game's most effective training secrets. This comprehensive, sport-specific training program will help you hit, throw, and run like an all-star. It features 85 exercises and drills, 10 training workouts, and 4 sample 12-week training programs.

208 pages • ISBN 0-87322-886-3

To request more information or to place your order,
U.S. customers call **TOLL-FREE 1-800-747-4457.**
Customers outside the U.S. use the appropriate
telephone number/address shown in the front of this book.

HUMAN KINETICS
The Premier Publisher for Sports & Fitness
P.O. Box 5076, Champaign, IL 61825-5076
www.humankinetics.com

2335

2/00